Scripture says, "My people are destroyed for lack of knowledge" (Hos. 4:6, *NIV*). The enemy of our souls is working overtime to pollute the very fabric of our culture. Many Christians are being swept away, unaware of Satan's devices to rob them of their peace and joy and the well-being of their homes. Like a hidden iceberg that tears a hole in a ship below the waterline, these pollutants can tear gaping holes in homes that will threaten to sink them. In this knowledgeable and biblical presentation, Chuck Pierce and Rebecca Sytsema skillfully instruct us in how we can have homes that are filled with God's presence and that are free from the sometimes subtle ways they can become polluted.

CHRIS HAYWARD
PRESIDENT, CLEANSING STREAM MINISTRIES

Protecting Your Home from Spiritual Darkness is a must-read for sincere Christians. Chuck Pierce demystifies a topic that is often viewed as superstitious or imbalanced. Regardless of whether you are well versed in the concept of spiritual warfare or just beginning to understand it, this book lays a clear foundation that will help you win the important battles in your life. For me, the acid test of this book's value is that its principles helped me during a cycle of sickness and depression that had attacked my family for years. Now it is your turn. Dare to believe that you can break through into realms of victory.

HARRY R. JACKSON, JR.
COAUTHOR, *HIGH-IMPACT AFRICAN-AMERICAN CHURCHES*
SENIOR PASTOR, HOPE CHRISTIAN CHURCH
WASHINGTON, D.C.

What is a spiritual housecleaning? Chuck Pierce tells us why and how to cleanse our homes in ways that some of us may never have considered before. I recommend *Protecting Your Home from Spiritual Darkness* as a must-read, must-do book.

QUIN SHERRER

COAUTHOR, *A WOMAN'S GUIDE TO SPIRITUAL WARFARE*

The devil is crafty and he will blindside you with his evil plans as much as he can. This book shows you how to unmask his footholds in your home and break their power once and for all.

C. PETER WAGNER

AUTHOR, *CHANGING CHURCH* AND *WHAT THE BIBLE SAYS ABOUT SPIRITUAL WARFARE*
CHANCELLOR, WAGNER LEADERSHIP INSTITUTE

PROTECTING YOUR HOME FROM SPIRITUAL DARKNESS

CHUCK D. PIERCE
REBECCA WAGNER SYTSEMA

Chosen

a division of Baker Publishing Group
Minneapolis, Minnesota

© 2000, 2004 by Chuck D. Pierce and Rebecca Wagner Sytsema

Published by Chosen Books
11400 Hampshire Avenue South
Bloomington, Minnesota 55438
www.chosenbooks.com

Chosen Books is a division of
Baker Publishing Group, Grand Rapids, Michigan

Chosen Books edition published 2014
ISBN 978-0-8007-9697-6

Revised edition. Previously published by Regal Books.
Originally published as *Ridding Your Home of Spiritual Darkness* by Wagner Publications, 2000.

Printed in the United States of America

Library of Congress Control Number: 2014955968

Unless otherwise indicated, Scripture quotations are from the New King James Version. Copyright © 1982 by Thomas Nelson, Inc. Used by permission. All rights reserved.

Scripture quotations labeled NIV are from the Holy Bible, New International Version®. NIV®. Copyright © 1973, 1978, 1984, 2011 by Biblica, Inc.™ Used by permission of Zondervan. All rights reserved worldwide. www.zondervan.com

Names of certain people referred to in illustrations have been changed, but the stories are factual.

14 15 16 17 18 19 20   7 6 5 4 3 2 1

CONTENTS

Chapter One 9
Spiritual Life, Liberty and Freedom

Chapter Two 18
Becoming Aware of Spiritual Darkness

Chapter Three 25
The Jewelry Box

Chapter Four 38
Spiritual Discernment

Chapter Five 47
A Demonic Foothold in the Land

Chapter Six 60
Overthrowing Generational Curses

Chapter Seven 71
Protecting Our Children from Spiritual Darkness

Chapter Eight 84
Ten Steps to Protecting Your Home from Spiritual Darkness

Appendix A 95
Prayer of Release for Freemasons and Their Descendants

Appendix B 107
Recommended Reading

CHAPTER ONE

SPIRITUAL LIFE, LIBERTY AND FREEDOM

The loud crash of thunder jerked Cathy from her troubled thoughts. Pulling the curtain aside, she peered out at the ominous clouds that had suddenly filled the Texas sky. The turbulent weather only served as a dark reminder of Cathy's own life as a fresh wave of the all-too-familiar depression seemed to overcome her once again. She could barely move under the weight of her own cloud that had nothing to do with the summer thunderstorm.

Cathy often suffered from bouts of deep, overwhelming depression. Despite counseling and prayer, we could not seem to discover the source of her constant gloom. As I was visiting with her one day, she asked me about a Greek statue that had been given to her by her former husband. She wondered if perhaps that statue had something to do with her depression. I agreed that the statue had to go, but I knew deep within my spirit that it was not linked to her suffering. Even so, I knew that something in her house was not right. I knew that some *thing* was connected to the dark shadow that hung over her emotions. I began walking through the house praying, "Lord, show me anything in this home that is representing Cathy's depression."

We looked at many antiques she had collected throughout the years. While antiques are often laden with demonic oppression, I knew that none of these objects was the problem. Then the Lord led me over to a glass bookcase. I knew in my spirit that there was something inside that needed to go. I reached up to the top shelf and pulled out a copy of the handbook for thirty-second-degree Masons. Cathy had no idea where the book had come from or that it was in her home. I knew that the book had to be destroyed, so we built a fire and burned it. That act was a turning point in Cathy's life. It set in motion a chain of events that led to the breaking of a Masonic curse in her bloodline. As the curse was broken, the gripping, overwhelming depression that had been Cathy's constant companion completely let go of her mind, and she has walked in freedom ever since. Finding that book was a key to exposing Satan's stronghold over her emotions. Destroying that book was an act of obedience that led to the eventual dismantling of that stronghold and to the liberty that Cathy enjoys today.

What happened to Cathy? How did I know what object needed to go? Were any demonic forces attached to the book? What did Cathy's bloodline have to do with her suffering? We seek to answer these and many other questions concerning how demonic forces work within our own homes. It is our prayer that this book will help you determine any spiritual housecleaning you may need to do in order to protect your home from spiritual darkness.

Understanding Spiritual Life

The thief does not come except to steal, and to kill, and to destroy. I have come that they may have life, and that they may have it more abundantly (John 10:10).

Jesus' words in this passage are not only a great comfort to His followers, but they also are a profound key to understanding the spiritual war in which we as Christians find ourselves. There is a thief who has come to steal, kill and destroy. He is the enemy of our souls, and it is important that we are wise to his schemes.

> if we do not understand spiritual life, we will not be able to see where death has established itself in our homes.

The real issue in understanding how Satan works to bring death is to have an understanding of spiritual life. If we do not understand spiritual life, we will not be able to see where death has gained access and established itself in our homes.

The "life" that Jesus has come to give us is translated from the Greek word *zoe*, which means to be possessed of vitality; to have life active and vigorous; to be devoted to God; to be blessed; to be among the living (not lifeless or dead); to enjoy real life, true life worthy of the name; to pass life on to others; to be fresh, strong, efficient, active, powerful; to be endless in the kingdom of God.[1] Furthermore, Jesus tells us that He has come to give us this rich existence in abundance, which means excessive, overflowing, surplus, over and above, more than enough, profuse, extraordinary, more than sufficient, superior, more remarkable, more excellent.[2] Life means movement. Any time the "life" of Jesus or the Holy Spirit quits moving within our lives, death begins its process. Death is the opposite of life. Therefore, we must be aware of anything that produces death within us.

The abundant life that Christ brings is not a promise of a fairy tale in which, as we live happily ever after, we find continual joy in our perfect life. In fact, the Bible clearly states that the opposite is true: "In the world you will have tribulation" (John 16:33). However, that verse goes on to say, "but be of good cheer, I have overcome the world." The apostle Paul takes it one step further by saying, "We also glory in tribulations, knowing that tribulation produces perseverance; and perseverance, character; and character, hope" (Rom. 5:3-4).

Because of our covenant relationship with God, even in times of tribulation, suffering or loss, we have the promise of abundant, *zoe* life. According to Isaiah 61, Jesus is anointed to heal the brokenhearted, proclaim liberty to the captives and give beauty for ashes, the oil of joy for mourning and a garment of praise for the spirit of heaviness. Such promises are the heritage of God's children. Our joy does not come from a perfect, pain-free life but rather from a peace that surpasses all understanding—from an intimate relationship with the author of *zoe* life (see Phil. 4:7).

Defining Liberty and Freedom

Part of the *zoe* life that we as Christians enjoy includes liberty and freedom. Liberty is defined as freedom from control, interference, obligation, restriction, external or foreign rule.[3] Freedom is defined as immunity, exemption and the power to enjoy all the privileges or special rights of citizenship.[4] Jesus lived, died and rose again to bring us liberty from the bondages of death, hell and the grave—that is, freedom from control, interference, obligation, restriction or the rule of Satan. Additionally, Jesus' shed blood gives us freedom to come before God with immunity and exemption from sin, and the power to enjoy all the privileges and special rights of heavenly citizenship.

The Indwelling and Empowering Work of the Holy Spirit

The very basis of experiencing *zoe* life is the ministry of the Holy Spirit to each and every one of us. As Robert Heidler, my own pastor for many years, writes in his book *Experiencing the Spirit*:

> The indwelling Spirit is the Spirit of Jesus living in the hearts of His people, sent to give them new hope, new love, new peace, new joy and new direction. This ministry is foundational to everything else in the Christian life. Through the indwelling Spirit we are *sealed* in Christ and given an inner assurance that we belong to Him (see 2 Cor. 1:22).
>
> Why would the Spirit of God want to live inside people like you and me? He lives in our hearts to enable us to

live life on a new level. He is working to change us from the inside out, so that we may become more like Jesus.[5]

Every Christian, at the time he or she accepted Christ, received the indwelling of the Holy Spirit. We know this is true because we are called "the temple of the Holy Spirit" (1 Cor. 6:19). It comes with Christianity. However, as Heidler goes on to point out, being empowered by the Holy Spirit is another matter.

> The *indwelling* ministry of the Spirit is automatic. . . . He came and took up residence within your heart at the moment of your salvation. In contrast, the *empowering* of the Spirit is seldom automatic, usually coming instead in response to prayer (emphasis added).[6]

Empowering of the Spirit is just as much a part of *zoe* life as indwelling of the Spirit.

No demonic force will ever comply with our commands to be gone without spiritual power backing us up.

Why is this important to the subject at hand—protecting your home from spiritual darkness? It is because we need the empowering work of the Spirit in order to wage warfare against the enemy. No demonic force will ever comply with our commands to be gone without spiritual power backing us up. The empowering work of the Spirit gives us the authority we need to evict demons from our homes and lives.

Cooperating with the Holy Spirit

The empowering of the Holy Spirit is not automatic; rather, it is one that we must pursue. Therefore, we need to learn ways to cooperate with what the Holy Spirit is longing to do. Here are eight principles outlining how to live a life prepared to receive empowerment:

1. Meditating in the Word of God. Mary pondered (meditated on) what the Holy Spirit spoke to her about the birth of Jesus, and it became a part of her until she brought it to birth and watched it grow to maturity and into the fullness of God's plan. The book of Joshua instructs us to meditate in God's Word day and night (see 1:8). If we read the Word without giving it any thought, when does God have the opportunity to give us any revelation on what we have read or show us how to apply it to our lives? How can prayer flow out of a passage that we don't understand? We need to be like Mary and allow God's Word to become a part of us.

2. Praying. My life is prayer. I would rather commune with God than with anyone else. Prayer is simply communicating with God; He longs to communicate with us. It is when we pray that the channels to God are open—both ways. He commands us to devote ourselves to prayer (see Col. 4:2). To neglect prayer is to neglect God Himself. When we fail to pray, we break that all-important commandment of loving God with all our heart, soul and mind (see Matt. 22:37-38).

3. Fasting. For the Christian, fasting is essential, because many times we cannot gain the revelation we need for our next step without it. Fasting removes spiritual clutter and puts us in a better position to hear God. Through fasting, we give up something temporal to receive something eternal. Fasting is not a magical formula to manipulate God, yet even Jesus agreed that there are some things that simply cannot be accomplished without fasting (see Matt. 17:19-21; Mark 9:26-29).

4. Giving. Giving is the very heart of God. We are called to multiply what God gives us, yet we cannot do this without becoming givers as well as receivers. Instead of receiving and giving, we often operate in a lack, or poverty, mentality. We must overcome our fear of not having enough or of not being worthy of what God has given us. Fear of such things can keep us from giving. Instead, we need to allow God to lead us into freedom as receivers and as givers.

> Anything that God has ordained us to accomplish is going to be met with resistance from our enemy.

5. Warring. Anything that God has ordained us to accomplish is going to be met with resistance from our enemy. In order to reach our full potential in God, we must learn warfare. Sometimes, however, it is not as aggressive as it sounds. For example, each of these eight disciplines is a form of warfare, because each thwarts the enemy's plans to steal God's best from us.

6. Worshiping. Worship is that place where we can enter into an intimacy with God. It is not just about singing songs, although music can be a catalyst for expressing deep worship to the Lord. Worship is a lifestyle of focusing our mind and heart on God and all He is. It is a response to all He has done for us. It is a fragrant, flowering offshoot of our covenant relationship with Him.

7. Working. I love to spend as much time as I can each day in prayer. But there is more than prayer. There is a time to get up off your knees and do something. We can pray all day, but eventually we have to realize that God will come to us and show us what He wants us to do. Many times we can speak to the mountain (see Matt. 17:20), but at other times we must dig through it to get to the other side. I call that spiritual work.

8. Resting. While God labored six days, He rested on the seventh. He commands us to do the same in the Ten Commandments (see Exod. 20:8-10). It must be a big issue since it made the top 10!

In our book *Possessing Your Inheritance*, we go into more detail on each of these eight principles. For now, however, it is enough that we are aware of these principles and understand that as we follow them, we are allowing the Holy Spirit to empower us with what we need to defeat the enemy within our homes.

Notes
1. James Strong, *The New Strong's Exhaustive Concordance of the Bible* (Nashville, TN: Thomas Nelson, 1990), refs. 2198 and 2222.
2. Ibid., ref. 4053.
3. *The American Heritage Dictionary of the English Language*, 4th ed., s.v. "liberty."
4. Ibid., s.v. "freedom."
5. Robert D. Heidler, *Experiencing the Spirit* (Ventura, CA: Renew Books, 1998), pp. 51, 54. [Italics in original.]
6. Ibid., p. 88.

CHAPTER TWO

BECOMING AWARE OF SPIRITUAL DARKNESS

If we are supposed to be partakers of *zoe* life and live in the liberty and freedom described in chapter 1, why do so many Christians (like Cathy) suffer from oppression, fear, low self-image, depression, uncontrollable sin patterns and other bondages that produce death rather than life?

The two main reasons why Christians do not enjoy the *zoe* life that God has promised are (1) sin and (2) Satan. We will deal more with the issues of sin—both personal and generational—in later chapters. Here, let's take a look at Satan and the forces he uses to steal the fullness out of our lives.

In *Warfare Prayer*, C. Peter Wagner writes:

> Satan's central task and desire is to prevent God from being glorified. Whenever God is not glorified in a person's life, in a church, in a city or in the world as a whole, Satan has to that degree accomplished his objective. . . . Satan's primary objective is to prevent God from being glorified by keeping lost people from being saved. . . . Satan's secondary objective is to make human beings and human society as miserable as possible in this present life.[1]

How does Satan accomplish these goals? He does whatever it takes to veer us away from God's path. As C. S. Lewis so aptly shows in *The Screwtape Letters*, our enemy's number one tactic is deception. He is a deceiver—the father of lies (see John 8:44). He prowls about looking for the right moment to pounce on us (see 1 Pet. 5:8). He takes advantage of every opportunity we give to him, but he is not omnipresent. So how is it that Satan manages to make so many of us miserable in this present life? He delegates.

At the enemy's disposal is a vast demonic host whose assignment is to see that Christians never reach their full potential while on Earth. In so doing, they have not only succeeded in causing us distress and grief, but they also have succeeded in keeping us from fulfilling the destiny that God has for us in this lifetime. God has a purpose—a great destiny for each and every one of us. This destiny is purposed to cause us to live *zoe* life, as well as designed to advance the kingdom of God on Earth. Getting us off course is, therefore, well worth Satan's efforts. He can steal *zoe* life from us and thwart God's purpose for our lives simultaneously.

Clever Disguises?

While there are many ways that demonic forces can oppress God's people, this book is written to help us discover how these forces gain a foothold within our own homes. As a first step, we must understand that demons use clever disguises to keep us ignorant of their work in our lives. As Noel and Phyl Gibson write in *Evicting Demonic Intruders,* "Demons cover their existence by deception, so that people concentrate on what they see, or how they feel, and overlook spiritual causes."[2]

Noel and Phyl Gibson go on to list four reasons why Christians may be unaware of demonic activity (I have added a fifth):

1. Fear of demons causes people to deny their existence.
2. Lack of spiritual discernment.
3. Most modern preaching and teaching avoids the subject of demonic activity.
4. First-century faith has largely been replaced by twentieth-century rationalism.[3]
5. Our Western mind-set keeps us from validating that which cannot be explained through scientific study.

Do objects have power? There is really nothing in an object itself. However, as believers, we must understand that there is often an invisible spiritual force behind a visible object. This is called the law of double reference. Many times in the Bible the Lord deals with a person or thing and asks us to look deeper into the spiritual force behind that person or thing. For instance, we find this in Isaiah 14 where the prophet Isaiah addresses the king of Babylon, and then we find references made to Lucifer. We find the same situation in Ezekiel 28. This is one way that demons operate. Paul writes, "We do not look at the things which are seen, but at the things which are not seen. For the things which are seen are temporary, but the things which are not seen are eternal" (2 Cor. 4:18). Paul implies that there is more we need to be aware of than that which we can perceive with our five natural senses.

Demons are masters of disguise.

Demons are masters of disguise. They can inhabit people, objects, portions of land or whole territories, depending on their purpose. They do not care *what* they inhabit, as long as they can accomplish their assigned objectives. They can gain access through sin, trauma, victimization, witchcraft, occult practices or cursing. While we do not want to become fascinated with demons, we must become aware of what they are and how they operate in order to keep our own homes free from spiritual darkness.

Haunted Houses?

When my coauthor, Rebecca Sytsema, met her husband, Jack, he asked her to come over to the apartment he was renting from the seminary he attended in order to pray. He reported that there was always a heavy, oppressive feeling inside the apartment. He didn't like being there at all. He knew the problem was spiritual and needed prayer.

When they arrived at the apartment, Jack gave Rebecca a quick tour and they began praying. An ominous feeling descended on them both. It was as if a dark shroud draped itself over the room. Suddenly, the microwave (which had not been in use) began beeping, the answering machine began making strange noises—rewinding itself and playing old, erased messages—and the lights began to flicker on and off—all within a matter of seconds, and all without explanation. Jack and Rebecca began praying harder!

Within a few minutes, a neighbor (also a seminary student), stormed down the stairs, pounded on the door and yelled a string of obscenities at Jack for causing the mysterious electrical fluctuations that were apparently affecting the whole building. There had been no history of electrical problems in the building and certainly no way for that man to know that anything was going on in Jack's apartment. Without a doubt, Jack and Rebecca had stirred up demonic forces that would have preferred to remain incognito.

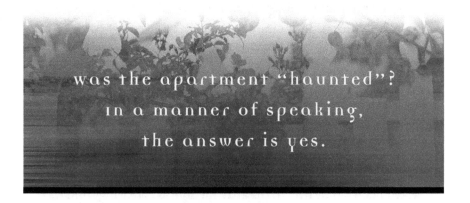

was the apartment "haunted"?
in a manner of speaking,
the answer is yes.

In the name of Jesus, Jack took authority as the legal tenant of that apartment and commanded the spirits to leave. By the leading of the Holy Spirit, he repented for any past sins that had been committed there. He anointed the doors and windows with oil and consecrated the apartment to the Lord. By the time they were done praying, great peace filled his home. Jack reported that he got his first good night's sleep since moving in several months earlier. A few weeks later, Jack sensed that the spirits were trying to regain residence. He and two other friends prayed through the apartment once again, and he had no further spiritual trouble for the remaining time he lived in that apartment.

Was the apartment "haunted"? In a manner of speaking, the answer is yes. It was not haunted by ghosts of human beings but rather by demonic forces whose job was to cloud the air with oppressive darkness. What better place to set up camp than in seminary housing where tomorrow's Christian leaders are supposed to receive training for ministry?

Does Your Home Need Prayer?

There is always a great deal of benefit in praying through a home for the purpose of consecrating it or setting it apart for the Lord. By doing this, you may or may not encounter spiritual darkness that needs to be dealt with. Yet there are indicators as to whether a home needs to be cleansed of spiritual darkness. The following list might indicate symptoms of a spiritually polluted atmosphere that requires spiritual cleansing:

- Sudden chronic illness
- Recurrent bad dreams and nightmares
- Insomnia or unusual sleepiness
- Behavioral problems
- Relational problems—continual fighting, arguing and misinterpreted communication
- Lack of peace
- Restless, disturbed children
- Unexplained illnesses or bondage to sin

- Ghosts or demonic apparitions (to which young children are particularly susceptible)
- Poltergeists (the movement of physical objects by demons)
- Foul, unexplainable odors
- Atmospheric heaviness, making it hard to breathe
- Continual nausea and headaches[4]

If you are experiencing any of these things on an ongoing basis, ask the Lord to reveal any spiritual darkness that may be in your home. Remember that Jesus gives us authority over these beings; He is far greater than any force that might come against you. There is no need to fear. Becoming aware of the demonic and how it may be affecting you is the first step to protecting your home from spiritual darkness.

Notes

1. C. Peter Wagner, *Warfare Prayer* (Ventura, CA: Regal Books, 1992), p. 61.
2. Noel and Phyl Gibson, *Evicting Demonic Intruders* (West Sussex, England: New Wine Press, 1993), p. 47.
3. Ibid., pp. 48-49.
4. Alice and Eddie Smith, *Spiritual Housecleaning* (Ventura, CA: Regal Books, 2003), p. 48.

THE JEWELRY BOX

My wife had to be crazy! What other explanation could there be for want-
ing to destroy a beautiful—and valuable—jewelry box? There was noth-
ing wrong with that box. How ridiculous! How wasteful!

Such were my thoughts on the day my wife, Pam, came home
from a prayer meeting and told me that her jewelry box had to
go. Little did I know that the Lord would use that jewelry box
to deliver me from a covetous, greedy spirit *and* teach me the
truth about demonic forces' inhabiting objects.

It happened several years ago. Pam was enjoying a spiritual
revival in her life. During that time, she and six other ladies decided to meet together for seven weeks to pray that their husbands
would come into a deeper spiritual walk and to experience renewal

in their own lives. In the sixth week, a friend who was a missionary to China came to the prayer meeting. She began to discuss how demonic forces could inhabit objects in order to bring spiritual darkness into a home. Having lived in China, this missionary had a different approach to spiritual issues than those of us with a Western mind-set. Her perspective made sense to Pam.

When Pam came home after that meeting, she recounted what the missionary told them. She told me that she could not stop thinking about a large, beautiful jewelry box from Thailand that her father had given her. The jewelry box was decorated with dragons, pagodas and buddhas—all kinds of images that she knew did not bring glory to God. The more she thought about it, the more she felt the box had to go.

i was aware of spiritual darkness,
but i had no idea that demons
could attach themselves to objects.

I thought she was totally off the wall! I was aware of spiritual darkness, but I had no idea that demons could attach themselves to objects. I told her that she was crazy for thinking that anything spiritual was linked to that jewelry box. I also reminded her that the box was a gift, and it was worth a lot of money. Why would we want to destroy a valuable object? My wife immediately submitted to me and did not mention it anymore.

Three weeks later, Pam and I were in some friends' home attending a prayer meeting. During that meeting, the Spirit of God spoke to me and said, "You have caused your wife to rebel against My will for her life, and I hold you accountable!" Immediately, I knew the Lord was talking about the jewelry box. He had revealed to Pam that she needed to destroy it, and I stopped her from obeying Him! At that moment, a deep fear of the Lord came over me. I knew that as soon as we got home, I had to take full responsibility for what I had done and burn that jewelry box myself.

When we got home, I immediately set a fire in the fireplace. I did not know exactly what I was doing, but I knew I had to do it. When I placed the jewelry box in the fireplace, a strange, eerie wind began to blow and stir all around the living room. The wind was not coming from outside. Something was generating it from within our home! The inexplicable wind blew so hard that it knocked a lamp clear off the wall. Not knowing exactly what I was dealing with, I became frightened.

At that time, there was a woman in our church who I knew understood spiritual things. So I called her, told her what was happening and asked her what to do. She began to pray for me over the phone. She told me to read some Scriptures and command any evil presence linked with that jewelry box to leave our home. When I did so, the Lord spoke to me and said, "I am delivering you from covetousness and the love of money!"

Once I was liberated from that particular demonic force in my life, it was as if my eyes were opened to many issues within our home that were linked with other evil forces. Freedom began to come to us in incredible ways—not only freedom, but spiritual revelation.

What Did the Jewelry Box Represent?

What did the jewelry box have to do with covetousness and the love of money? At first it had nothing to do with it. The engraved images of dragons, pagodas and buddhas on the jewelry box were not glorifying to God. They were carven images of gods and creatures worshiped in the Thai culture, which was why the Holy Spirit convicted Pam to get rid of it.

When I stood in the way of ridding our home of unclean images on the basis of the box's monetary value, my own covetousness and greed, and the demonic forces that had been in my family concerning those issues, became linked with the jewelry box. In other words, it was simply a matter of my unwillingness to obey God and destroy something of value that made the object a symbol of an evil force in my life. When the fear of the Lord came on me and I chose to destroy the box, regardless of its value, the act broke the back of a demonically inspired love of money that had been passed down to me from my father (see chapter 6 for more on generational iniquity). God delivered my home of an unclean object, *and* He delivered me of a covetous spirit at the same time.

Objects that we may possess, although not inherently wrong, often represent a demonic stronghold in our lives. The jewelry box was just that kind of item in my life. It had images on it that needed to be cleansed from my house. Yet even if the box hadn't had those images, my unwillingness to give it up due to its value showed a much deeper problem that was, in fact, a demonic stronghold of covetousness and the love of money.

The love of money is a major issue, especially in American society. It is the only sin of the flesh that is "hard-core idolatry," a term coined by C. Peter Wagner. Referring to Luke 16:13, "You cannot serve both God and Money" (*NIV*), Wagner writes:

Covetousness is allegiance to a false god named Mammon. . . . It is correct to capitalize "Money" or "Mammon" because it is a proper name. Mammon is a person, not a thing or an urge or an attitude. . . . When

Jesus mentioned Mammon, it was in the context of not being able to serve two masters. Serving any supernatural master in the demonic world, like Mammon, is hardcore idolatry.[1]

This was the allegiance that the jewelry box came to represent in my life. When I chose to obey God and get rid of the jewelry box, the demonic force of Mammon lost its grip in my life, and I was delivered.

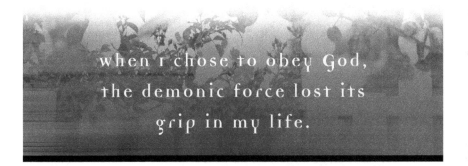

when i chose to obey God, the demonic force lost its grip in my life.

When Mammon Interferes with Obedience

Have you ever noticed your dollar bill? I once was ministering at a deliverance conference on the issue of objects and how many times evil characters are imbedded in objects. The evil eye is right there on the dollar bill. I'll explain more about the evil eye in chapter 7. Does that mean we burn all of our dollar bills? Well, of course not. But it does make us aware that there is a snare to money. When the Lord was ready to send the people of Israel into the Promised Land, He had many warnings for them. He knew they would be in spiritual war with the god Mammon. Mammon can rule the economic system, which allows demonic forces to be involved in the administration, transfer and distribution of wealth. When you study Canaanite history, you find that the ruling god of the Canaanites was Mammon. The assignment or mission that

Joshua and the tribes of Israel had to accomplish was to transfer wealth from all of the inhabitants of that region into God's covenant, kingdom plan. Therefore, Mammon had to be defeated, and the wealth held by its false worship transferred.

> No one can serve two masters; for either he will hate the one and love the other, or else he will be loyal to the one and despise the other. You cannot serve God and mammon (Matt. 6:24).

When Provision Becomes a Golden Calf

Provision is necessary for our lives to be functional in our world. However, the Lord says to be in the world but not of the world (see 1 John 2:15-17). When the Israelites left Egypt, God prompted the Egyptians to give them all kinds of goods. Exodus 12:36 reads, "And the LORD had given the people favor in the sight of the Egyptians, so that they granted them what they requested. Thus they plundered the Egyptians." Imagine the masters of these slaves filling their hands with silver and gold. This is an example of what the Lord still wishes to do for His children as He breaks us out of the system in which we live and points us toward the Covenant blessings He has throughout the earth. God gave Moses a detailed plan for the people. However, the people did not wait on Moses. Instead of waiting patiently, as instructed, they grew impatient. Therefore, they took all of the provision God had provided them and, in their discouragement, wandered back to the other gods from whom they had been liberated.

> And he [Aaron] received the gold from their hand, and he fashioned it with an engraving tool, and made a molded calf. Then they said, "This is your god, O Israel, that brought you out of the land of Egypt!" (Exod. 32:4).

Not only was this molded bull calf a familiar god that had been in Egypt, but it also was worshiped in Canaan through the religious system that had been erected in Canaanite worship. When we do not offer God His portion and make our provision holy before Him, we open ourselves up to the operation of the evil eye working over our finances. The evil eye aligns with our idolatry, and our idolatry aligns with Mammon. Thus, we find ourselves under the control of this false god.

While covetousness may be the only sin of the flesh that is hard-core idolatry, it is not the only thing that may represent a demonic stronghold in your life. Take lust, for example. Perhaps there is something in your home from a past romantic relationship (maybe a gift, some old love letters or hidden photos), and you are now married to another person. A demonic stronghold of lust or of inappropriate love can easily attach itself to that item. Destroying whatever it is will help you overcome the enemy's grip in that area of your life. It will help you leave the past behind and move forward into God's destiny for you and your family.

Knowing what might represent a demonic stronghold in our lives or what objects are not glorying to God often takes spiritual discernment. In chapter 4, we will look at what discernment is and how to use it to protect our homes from spiritual darkness.

Why Should We Take a Look at What We Own?

The jewelry box brings up two distinct instances of objects that need to be dispatched in order to protect our homes from spiritual darkness: (1) objects that do not bring glory to God; and (2) objects that represent demonic strongholds in our own lives. Let's look at each one of these instances.

There are several instances in the Bible when disaster occurred because of objects. One instance is when Rachel died while giving birth to Benjamin (see Gen. 35). What was the result of her premature death? In Genesis 31, Jacob fled from Laban. When Laban caught up with him and accused him of stealing some household gods, Jacob said, "With whomever you find your gods, do not let him live. In the presence of our brethren, identify what I have of yours and take it with you" (v. 32). Jacob did not know that Rachel had stolen the household gods and put them in her camel's saddle. When Laban was searching for the objects linked with his idolatrous form of worship, Rachel pretended to be in her monthly period and actually sat on the household gods. She was not willing to let go of an old form of worship linked with her father. As a result, she died prematurely.

A similar story is told in Joshua 7. Israel experienced defeat in the battle of Ai, which occurred immediately after its great victory in Jericho. Achan, despite God's warning not to take any cursed things, took and hid several of the forbidden objects. As a result, Israel was defeated. In the end, Achan and his whole family were destroyed because of his sin.

On the other hand, freedom occurred when believers in Ephesus brought their idolatrous items and objects linked with magic and sorcery, and burned them in the middle of the city (see Acts 19). This was a key to one of the greatest revivals and awakenings recorded in the Bible.

The Problem with Objects

Once we become aware of spiritual darkness, we can begin looking around in our homes and see what we own that does not bring glory to God. What we mean by this phrase is something that, by its very nature, can attract or be inhabited by darkness. Here are five categories of such objects:

1. Foreign Gods. "You shall not make for yourself any carved image, or any likeness of anything that is in heaven above, or that is in the earth beneath, or that is in the water under the earth" (Deut. 5:8). In this passage, the second of the Ten Commandments, "a carved image" refers to any tangible object that represents an idol, god or demonic figure. Not only is this a welcome mat for demonic activity, but also God hates it. Though it may be out of ignorance, it is surprising to realize how many Christians have such items in their homes.

These objects include buddhas (as was on Pam's jewelry box); Hindu images; fertility gods or goddesses (or any type of god or goddess); Egyptian images; Greek gods; gargoyles; kachina dolls, totem poles or any other Native American figures that depict or glorify a spirit or demonic being; evil depictions of creatures such as lions, dogs, dragons or cats (or any other creature made with demonic distortions); or any other image of a person, idol, god or demonic figure that is considered an object of worship or spiritual power in any culture in the world.

On trips, many people collect these types of artifacts as souvenirs without truly understanding their significance—much like the jewelry box that came from Thailand.

2. False Religions. Objects or materials related to false religions, such as Mormonism, Islam, Jehovah's Witness, Hinduism, Eastern religions, Christian Science, Native religions, Baha'i and so forth, need to be carefully evaluated. This includes instruction books on Yoga, transcendental meditation, mantras and so on.

3. Occult Objects. Anything related to the occult must be destroyed completely. These objects include Ouija boards; good luck charms; amulets; astrology items (including horoscopes); tarot cards; crystals; fetishes; water witching sticks; voodoo dolls; pagan symbols; crystal balls; any ritual item, such as a mask, a pyramid or an obelisk; any item obtained from occult or voodoo shops; any item related to black magic, fortune-telling, palmistry, demon worship, spirit guides, witchcraft, Satanism or New Age. None of these items or any other such item should have any place in the Christian home.

> Anything related to the occult must be destroyed completely.

4. Secret-Society Objects. Remember the story in chapter 1 about Cathy and the handbook for thirty-second-degree Masons? That book was connected to her depression. Secret societies, such as Freemasonry, Shriners, Eastern Star, Job's Daughters, Odd Fellows, Elks, Amaranth, DeMolay, Rainbow for Girls or Daughters of the Nile, often require their members to take oaths and go through initiation rituals, including pledging allegiance to various deities, which are completely contrary to God's Word. Because that is the case, demons can easily attach themselves to items, such as books, rings, aprons, regalia and memorabilia, that represent these societies. Additionally, because such items are often passed down through family lines, there is a generational issue that must be dealt with (see chapter 6).

5. Other Objects. Our homes may be filled with other items that do not bring glory to God and may attract demonic activity. These include games such as Masters of the Universe and Dungeons and Dragons, in addition to myriad demonic or violent video games; books and magazines devoted to fantasy; comic books, posters, movies or music with demonic, violent or sexual themes; pornography; illegal drugs; sensual art, books or "toys"; or a number of other things that are demonic, illegal, immoral or contrary to God's Word.

By allowing any of these types of things into our homes, we give the enemy a legal right to invade our lives in ways that he would otherwise not have access. As Cindy Jacobs would say, we have holes in our armor. In order to bring clarity into the process of deciding what might need to go, C. Peter Wagner encourages us to ask the following questions:

· Might this open me to direct demonic influence?
· Does this give any appearance of evil?
· Does this glorify God?[2]

Ethnic Culture Versus Kingdom Culture

A culture is the totality of socially transmitted behavior patterns, arts, beliefs, institutions and all other products of human work and thought. Culture is also the predominating attitudes and behavior that characterize the functioning of a group or organization.[3]

There are many objects in our lives that define the culture from which we come. Some objects are unique to a particular culture. Some things are just objects and do not represent any evil. Some objects are used in evil ways in one culture but are very harmless in another culture. Some objects are plain evil and unredeemable.

As Christians, we are part of the culture in which we are born; yet we also are part of God's kingdom culture that transcends racial, national and physical boundaries. We can appreciate much about our natural culture, such as food, holidays and some traditions, but we cannot ignorantly embrace everything. We must consider the cultural object, practice or whatever it may be and weigh it against the standards God sets in His kingdom culture.

A kingdom has a king. We must always represent our King in all that we do on Earth. Anything in our culture that is contrary to or falsely represents the King in our Kingdom, we must be willing to let go of or remove from our sphere of authority or home.

Because every kingdom has a culture, we want to be sure the culture of God's kingdom is overriding or sanctifying anything that is from our worldly culture. This does not require us to get rid of all the objects of our culture, but it does make us have a responsibility to see that those objects are brought under the sanctifying blood of the Lord Jesus Christ. If we do not do this, our conscience will be hindered and our vision will be blurred over God's plan for our lives. We should never let an object in our culture become a stumbling block to entering into a new dimension of God's kingdom.

We work very closely with Native Americans, or the host people of this land. Without the host people of a nation (any nation, not just the United States) coming unto their destined inheritance in God, the nation itself can never fully experience the plan of God.

There has been much discussion about Native artifacts, feathers, drums, dream catchers, jewelry and so on. Possessing such items usually becomes a matter of conscience. However, there are certain objects that were dedicated and used for occult purposes in our host culture. These objects were made solely for the purposes of evil or to gain illegal revelation from dark sources. These types of items will be a hindrance in a Christian walk. We must very carefully deal with objects that may be a stumbling block to our spiritual development, as well as to the spiritual development of new believers.

The Problem with Garments

In any culture, there are customs, traditions, values, laws, rules of supply, garments and dress. Some of these items are used in worship in different cultures. Therefore, we need to review very carefully all that we own when moving into the kingdom of God—especially items of worship and dress.

Your wardrobe can represent a season in your life. Zechariah 3 talks about how Satan accuses Joshua the high priest over his past. The Lord rebukes Satan, but then He does something else. He changes Joshua's clothing. He removes the filthy garments linked with his past and puts on new garments—"rich robes" (v. 4). He also puts a new turban on Joshua's head, which represents the new thought process of his mind for a new season.

I periodically clean out my closet. I find clothes that have emotional ties or inordinate affections with which I associate them. I may have clothes that do not represent the expression of my personality at that time or outdated garments. I also may find clothes that are linked with a season of grief in my life.

Remember in Ruth 3, Naomi made Ruth change her clothes. She was still wearing the clothes linked with Moab. These garments were filled with grief because of the loss of her husband. In other words, Naomi said, "Take off that widow's garment. We have to make a move to shift into our inheritance!"

Put off, concerning your former conduct, the old man which grows corrupt according to the deceitful lusts, and be renewed in the spirit of your mind, and that you put on the new man which was created according to God, in righteousness and true holiness (Eph. 4:22-24).

Clean out your closets! Change your clothes to reflect God and His kingdom in this season of your life!

Notes

1. C. Peter Wagner, *Hard-Core Idolatry: Facing the Facts* (Colorado Springs, CO: Wagner Publications, 1999), p. 17.

2. C. Peter Wagner, *Breaking Strongholds in Your City* (Ventura, CA: Regal Books, 1993), p. 65.

3. *The American Heritage Dictionary of the English Language*, 4th ed., s.v. "culture."

SPIRITUAL DISCERNMENT

"How do we know when we've prayed enough?" she asked me. The woman and her husband sat across from me, describing their situation in some detail. There was a piece of property that they owned. They regularly prayed over it, hoping to plant a church there some day. But they knew that something was wrong.

"Every time we set foot on that property, the hair on my arms stands up!" she explained. "We've prayed and prayed. How do we know when we've prayed enough?"

"It's very simple," I told her, "pray until the hair on your arms goes down!"

The Meaning of Spiritual Discernment

Spiritual discernment is the grace to see into the unseen. It is a gift *of the Spirit* to perceive what is *in the spirit*. Its purpose is to see into the nature of that which is veiled (emphasis added).[1]

This quote from Francis Frangipane is helpful in understanding what discernment is. It is something that we know by seeing with our spiritual eyes rather than with our physical eyes.

Gary Kinnaman defines it this way:

There are three kinds of spirits: evil spirits, human spirits, and heavenly spirits, including angels and the Spirit of God. The discerning of spirits is the ability to identify the kind of spirit that is the driving force behind a particular event, circumstance or thought. If it is determined that the spirit is an evil one, the discerning of spirits operating with precision can also identify the specific kind of evil spirit.[2]

There are some in the Body of Christ who have a gift of discernment. Those with a developed, mature gift are able to discern what the spiritual atmosphere of a place or around a person is more often and with more accuracy than most Christians. But the ability to discern spirits is not limited to those with "the gift." God can speak to any Christian through the Holy Spirit and give spiritual insight into any given situation. Spiritual discernment may seem like a complicated or difficult thing, but the fact is that discernment can be as simple as praying until the hair on your arms goes down. It's a matter of learning how to use the discernment God gives.

A Lamp unto My Feet

How do we learn how to have spiritual discernment? Discernment comes through knowing God. There are two main keys to knowing God: (1) God's Word; and (2) hearing by the spirit through prayer (see Heb. 5:14). They are both important factors to spiritual discernment.

> Through Your precepts I get understanding; therefore I hate every false way. Your word is a lamp to my feet and a light to my path (Ps. 119:104-105).

As we read and digest the Word of God, we develop important spiritual principles within us. These principles help illuminate the path that God sets before us; they act as a lamp unto our feet. For instance, by knowing the Word of God, we understand that we are not to have any carven images of idols in our homes (see chapter 3). That understanding helps us become

God wants to give us the discernment we need to protect our homes from spiritual darkness.

sensitive to seeing carven images of idols all around us, whether in our homes, in our places of work or wherever we may be.

I have developed a real aversion to any images of idols, false gods or the demonic, because I know how much God hates them. Just as Psalm 119 says, I gained understanding about such images through God's precepts (His Word), which helped me become aware of these kinds of images all around me. My understanding also has helped me set a rule about what I will not own, namely images of idols. God's Word has become a lamp unto my feet. From knowing God's Word, I can look at objects within my home and see what does not line up with the Bible. This is part of discernment.

The Voice of God

There are certain things we must discern, however, that are not as apparent as the image of an idol. These are spiritual issues; they must be discerned spiritually. We must hear from God in order to know what is going on, and the key to hearing God is prayer—two-way communication in which you speak to Him and He speaks to you.

Hearing the voice of God is not as difficult as some might think. I have found that many of God's people hear Him, but they have not perceived it as His voice. To perceive means to take hold of, feel, comprehend, grasp mentally, recognize, observe or become aware of something.[3] We must learn how to perceive God's voice and the prompting of the Holy Spirit.

God may speak to us through spiritual dreams (unusually vivid and detailed dreams that stick in our spirit), visions, visitations, a prophetic word, a conversation with a friend that brings revelation, a message we've heard or a feeling—like the woman whose hair stood up on her arms. When we hear from God, we suddenly know that we know something—a revelation takes place in our spirit. Our challenge is to sharpen our spiritual ears to hear God and to not write off what we hear as mere imagination. God *wants* to communicate with us. We must believe that.

Furthermore, God does not want us to be ignorant of how the enemy tries to ensnare us. He wants to give us the discernment we need to protect our homes from spiritual darkness.

Spiritual Boundaries

When we discern something that we believe is from the Lord, we must allow the Lord to show us what to do with the discernment. This fact became apparent in my own life not long after the jewelry box incident. From that time on, the Lord began to open my eyes to other objects in my home that were linked with demonic forces. My discernment was sharpening all the time.

One day, I was walking by our fireplace and saw a large ceramic cat that I had purchased some time before. It was a beautiful object with piercing blue eyes. The cat was worth a lot of money, but money was no longer an issue since my deliverance from the love of money when I destroyed the jewelry box. As I looked at the cat, I immediately discerned that witchcraft was linked to it. I then remembered that, out of my ignorance, I had purchased the cat in a voodoo shop in New Orleans when I was on a business trip. I began to see that this cat was linked with spiritism in my bloodline, which is why I was drawn into the voodoo shop in the first place and felt compelled to buy the cat (see chapter 6 for more information about this phenomenon). I knew the cat had to go. Because it was ceramic, I knew that it would not burn like the jewelry box. Nonetheless, I passed it through the fire and then smashed it (see Deut. 5:7).

In my zeal, I began to look around the house for other such objects. I found many ceramic cats that my wife had collected through the years. Because of my spiritual immaturity, I assumed that if the ceramic cat I bought was evil, all the other cats were evil, so I smashed them all. When Pam came home later that day, she asked what had happened to her cats. I explained to her what I had done. She just looked at me and said, "There was nothing wrong with my cats. It was *your* cat that had the problem. You have a choice. You can either replace the cats yourself or give me money to buy new ones."

She was absolutely right. My good discernment had run amuck! The problem was not ceramic cats in general; rather, the problem was one particular ceramic cat that I had purchased ignorantly in a voodoo shop. I did not heed the spiritual boundaries that should have been obvious. As a result, I got in a lot of trouble with my wife!

Along these same lines, I have seen some people get rid of everything that has feathers on it. Even though feathers can be used in occult activities, it does not mean that all feathers are wrong. We have birds that have feathers. As long as those birds are for our enjoyment, their feathers pose no problem. Yet if I use their feathers as objects in occult worship, then those particular feathers become a problem. The same is true of many Native American artifacts (see chapter 3).

Spiritual Authority

Spiritual boundaries are linked with authority. Each of us is given a sphere of authority in which we are free to operate (see 2 Cor. 10:13). When we move beyond that sphere of authority is when we run into real problems. Take the cats, for example. Even if there had been demons attached to my wife's ceramic cats, I did not have the authority to destroy them without her permission, because they simply did not belong to me.

I know many people who, upon learning the principles outlined in this book, made major mistakes because they did not understand their spiritual authority. Armed with discernment and the name of Jesus, they felt they could rid the world of demonic forces. That is just not so. We may begin to discern all kinds of problems, but we must understand that we are not free to deal with every problem we see—nor is it wise.

If you visit your mother's house, for example, and see that she has a statue of Buddha, and she is unwilling to get rid of it, you do not have the right either legally or spiritually to take her statue. It is beyond your spiritual authority. What you can do is pray and ask the Lord to reveal the principles outlined in this book to her. Maybe she would be willing to read this book. There may be other things you can do to help her understand, but taking what is not yours definitely crosses the line of authority, not to mention breaks one of the Ten Commandments—"You shall not steal" (Exod. 20:15). Any spirit attached to the statue can actually gain greater power because of the sin of stealing.

If your mother, on the other hand, asks you to get rid of the statue and pray for her, then she has given you the authority not only to destroy the statue but also to command any spirits attached to that statue to leave. In this case, she has extended spiritual authority for you to act on her behalf, and you are free to deal with the situation.

Ask the Lord to show you what your sphere of authority is before moving out in presumption and, thereby, making things worse than they were before!

A Gargoyle in the Attic

Some years ago, I was asked to pray over a building owned by some friends. Their business was located on the bottom floor, and some apartments occupied the top floor. The building had been plagued with many continual problems, including flooding. My friends had come to believe that there was a spiritual

problem, so they called me. When I entered the building, I immediately knew something was very wrong. The evil was so strong
that I couldn't breathe! Through discernment, I knew that there
was some object within the building that had demonic forces
attached to it, and I knew it was somewhere above us.

My friends trusted my discernment, and they spent $30,000
to tear out the ceiling in order to see what might be there. They
found nothing. I knew that, despite their great efforts, something

> The Lord revealed that the gargoyle
> had been planted as a fetish in
> order to curse the building.

had been missed. Some months later, as they were renovating the
building and having electrical work done, they discovered a
cement gargoyle hidden in one corner of the attic. I knew that
was what we had been looking for! The Lord revealed that the
gargoyle had been planted as a fetish in order to curse the building. We destroyed the gargoyle and prayed through the building,
dedicating it to the Lord. Since that time my friends have not
encountered any trouble with the building.

Planted Fetishes

A fetish is an object believed to have magical or spiritual powers,
or is an object linked with an abnormally obsessive preoccupation

or attachment or fixation.[4] These objects represent or are connected with some supernatural being. By possessing these
objects or having someone plant them in what we possess, they
can give place to demonic beings to operate through them.
Many times in past generations, fetishes were planted in the
ground.

Some people will discern that there is something wrong in
their land or house or even a car, but they can't see where the
problem is coming from. Items such as the gargoyle in the attic
are fetishes. Until these objects are removed, demon forces have
the right to hinder God's plan in that place. We rented a house
once that really had a problem in one room. My wife and daughter could both sense there was something wrong in that room.
I freaked out every time I walked in it. I finally walked into the
closet and looked up and saw an entry into the ceiling. When we
got up into the ceiling, we found evil magazines and parapher-
nalia. Once we removed the material, we anointed the room and
the portion of the attic above the room. The room was cleansed
from that day forward.

Notes
1. Francis Frangipane, *Discerning of Spirits* (Cedar Rapids, IA: Arrow Publications, 1991), p. 6.
2. Gary D. Kinnaman, *Overcoming the Dominion of Darkness* (Old Tappan, NJ: Chosen Books, 1990), pp. 133-134.
3. *The American Heritage Dictionary of the English Language,* 4th ed., s.v. "perceive."
4. Ibid., s.v. "fetish."

CHAPTER FIVE

A Demonic Foothold in the Land

Elaine awakened suddenly to the anguished screams of her son. *Not again!* she thought as she pulled on her bathrobe and wearily shuffled down the hall to Joey's room. She pushed the door open to find the familiar sight of her three-year-old son sobbing on his bed. She dropped onto the bed, gathered the small boy into her arms and stroked his head that was soaked with tears and sweat.

"It's okay, Joey," she whispered in his ear. "Mommy's here. No one will hurt you." She began to rock him back and forth as she had so many nights before, trying to calm him down. A full hour later, Elaine finally crawled into her own bed, but she could not fall asleep. She wondered why her son had not slept one full night since they had moved into this house, almost six months ago. He had slept well before, but something here was different.

Enough was enough. The next day Elaine called Joan, the pastor's wife, for counsel and prayer. Joan suggested that perhaps they needed to pray through Joey's room. She agreed to come over that afternoon. As the women began praying, Joan had a strong sense that something in the room was truly wrong—that there was an evil presence there.

As Joan prayed further, she began to see a picture of a young child being beaten in that room. She knew that the Lord was showing her why the evil presence lingered in Joey's room. Looking at Elaine, she said, "I believe that there may have been some kind of child abuse that took place in this room."

Stunned, Elaine began to explain to Joan that Joey's night terrors were often brought on by dreams of someone beating him. She had never understood this since neither she nor her husband had ever struck him with that kind of force. "What can we do?" Elaine asked.

Grabbing Elaine's hand, Joan kneeled by the bed and began asking God to forgive the sin of child abuse that had taken place in the room. Tears came to their eyes as they identified with the young child who had suffered in this place. After a few minutes of dealing with these revelations and asking God to cleanse the room, Joan rose to her feet, and with authority in her voice, she commanded the evil presence to leave the property and never return. At that moment, a great peace descended on the house. The room looked brighter. Elaine realized that for the first time since moving in, she felt totally at peace herself.

That night Joey slept well. Since praying through his room, the terror that plagued him never recurred. About a month after the incident, Elaine was visiting with her next-door neighbor who had lived there for several years. She asked about the family who had lived there before. Elaine's neighbor told her that she often heard yelling coming from the house and that on three occasions the police had to come break up the fights. Although the neighbor was not sure, she heard through the neighborhood grapevine that the authorities had removed the son from the home due to abuse suffered at the hands of his parents!

Understanding Land and Property

Up to this point, we have discussed the objects we own; however, part of protecting our homes from spiritual darkness also has to do with the land on which we live. In Elaine's story, we see that her young son was tormented by spiritual darkness unrelated to any object, or even to any sin in which Elaine had been involved. The land on which they lived, however, had been defiled through sin, which left an opening for demonic invasion that, until it was dealt with through prayer, continued to torment.

How can this be? Just as dark forces can inhabit an object, they also can inhabit land or places. In fact, some high-ranking principalities and powers can inhabit whole cities or territories. But if the earth is the Lord's (see Ps. 24:1), where do demons get the right to stake a claim to a particular part of the earth? The answer is through sin. Sin has a direct effect on land. We see this evidenced numerous times throughout the Bible.

In the story of Cain and Abel, for instance, God said to Cain, "What have you done? The voice of your brother's blood cries out to Me from the ground. So now you are cursed from the earth, which has opened its mouth to receive your brother's blood from your hand" (Gen. 4:10-11). Sin produces a curse in the land—in the physical ground where it occurs—and where there are curses, evil abounds.

Gaining a Foothold

The word "foothold" means a secure position that provides a base for further progress or advancement.[1] When the enemy gains a foothold, he has firmly established himself in a position from which he can progress with his evil schemes to kill, steal and destroy (see John 10:10). Let's look at Ephesians 4:25-27:

> Therefore, putting away lying, "Let each one of you speak truth with his neighbor," for we are members of one another. "Be angry, and do not sin": do not let the sun go down on your wrath, nor give place to the devil.

> First, we must understand how Satan can gain a foothold in our own lives. If we allow sin into our lives and do not confess it, we leave a door open, giving the enemy an opportunity to attack

If we allow sin into our lives and do not confess it, we leave a door open.

what is ours and to attack us. This verse in Ephesians talks about anger. Even though anger is an emotion and can be righteous, we see here that if we do not operate in a godly manner when we are angry, it can embed in our emotions and open the door to the enemy to gain a foothold. The same is true of any sin that has not been cleansed by the blood of Jesus. Sin that is not dealt with gives Satan a legal right into a situation, even in the life of a believer.

A great doctrinal debate throughout the history of Christendom has been the issue of demonic influence in the lives of true, born-again believers. Most theologians do not have a problem with the concept of Satan's right to tempt a Christian. But if Satan cannot gain some benefit into the lives of believers through that sin, why does he bother? Anyone with experience in the field of deliverance knows that Christians are prime targets for demonization, or a demonic foothold. This does not mean that the person is demon possessed, which means a demonic entity has full control; rather, the person is demonically influenced or tormented in a particular area of life. The opening for demonization is often sin—either personal or generational.[2]

Just as the enemy can gain a foothold into our lives through sin, he also can gain a foothold into land through sin that has been committed there. Back to Ephesians 4:25-27, the phrase, "do not . . . give place to the devil" means do not give him a foothold or opportunity. *Topos* is the Greek word for "place" in this verse. From *topos* we get the word "topographical," which means a literal place, locality or piece of land.[3] Sin gives the enemy a foothold—a secure position that provides a base for further progress or advancement—to *topos*—a literal place, locality or piece of land. From the physical place where Satan has a foothold, he seeks to do his three favorite things: steal, kill and destroy (see John 10:10).

Therefore, the issue with our homes is not just what we own but also what has occurred in our homes or on the land on which our homes were built. Has any sin occurred that gives the enemy a place there—a foothold? Remember the woman in chapter 4 whose hair stood up on her arms? She was discerning a problem on the land. She had found evidence of occult rituals having been performed there. The land was undoubtedly full of demonic forces that had gained a foothold as a result of the ungodly worship. No wonder her hair stood up!

Defiling the Land

While any sin can be an opening for demonic activity, there are certain sins that can defile (i.e., bring a foul, dirty, uncleanness to) the land. These sins leave the land cursed and particularly susceptible to demonic footholds:

1. Idolatry. God hates idolatry (see chapter 3). Just as the worship of God brings blessing upon the land, the worship of false gods brings curses.

2. Bloodshed. Earlier we mentioned the story of Cain and Abel. From this story, we see that bloodshed affected the very land on which the violence occurred. As the blood of violence penetrates the ground, "the prince of the power of the air" (Eph. 2:2) gains right into the land through the cursing caused by violence and bloodshed.

3. Immorality. This issue is one that we here in America must take seriously. "Immorality" has become a vague term and a non-issue for those in power. Our society has come to believe that anyone can do whatever is right in his or her own sight. But Satan knows that every immoral act opens up a greater legal right for him to infiltrate land and homes. With the advent of the Internet, there is even greater access to things like pornography and adult chat rooms. None of these things is benign. What is done in secret can bring serious consequences through defilement of those involved, as well as of the land on which their sin occurred.

4. Covenant Breaking. During the reign of King David, a great famine came on the land. When David inquired of the Lord concerning this famine, God said to him: "It is because of Saul and his bloodthirsty house, because he killed the Gibeonites" (2 Sam. 21:1). The Gibeonites were a group of people who had entered into covenant with Israel in the days of Joshua. This covenant guaranteed their safety. However, Saul broke the covenant with the Gibeonites by murdering many of them and planning for the massacre of the rest. As a result, famine came on the land as God removed His blessing and Satan was allowed access. The famine did not strike immediately but came when the new king came to power. Many of our homes in the United States have been built on land that was taken through broken treaties with Native Americans. Those broken treaties from years ago can defile and give the enemy a foothold on the land where we live today!

Wondering About the Cause

You may be wondering why demonic forces can torment a Christian in a place if the Christian did not do the sinning that gave those forces the legal right to establish a foothold in that place. Here is where you must understand the spiritual principle of remitting sin:

> And according to the law almost all things are purified with blood, and without shedding of blood there is no remission [of sin] (Heb. 9:22).

The principle is this: No sin is atoned for without the shedding of blood. It was a principle in the Old Testament; it was a principle in the New Testament; and it is still a principle today. The difference between the Old and New Testaments is Jesus. The blood that Jesus shed on the cross is what we can appropriate to remit or atone for sin, but we must appropriate it in order for the sin to be remitted. Until repentance has occurred and the blood of Jesus is applied, the sin—and thus Satan's legal right to a foothold—remains intact.

> Land that has been defiled through sin is like a soul that has been defiled through sin.

Land that has been defiled through sin is like a soul that has been defiled through sin. Without repentance and the appropriation of Jesus' blood, a place remains defiled and Satan has a right there. A Christian's taking control of a piece of property is *not* enough to rid it of spiritual darkness! Any demonic force that has a foothold in that place will continue to operate from that foothold until it is expelled through the remitting of whatever sin gave it the right in the first place.

Discovering Prayer Needs

First, you must know what to pray for. The very first step is, of course, to repent of any known sin you or someone else participated in—in your home or on your land. Beyond that, there are two ways of figuring out what needs prayer: (1) spiritual discernment and (2) research. We already discussed spiritual discernment. Remember the little boy, Joey, who was tormented by dreams of child abuse? There are many instances when you will not know the history of a place and must rely on the Lord to show you how to pray. One important question to ask while praying is, What is the fruit of the problem? In Joey's case, his dreams of child abuse were a major clue. The fruit was connected to the root. Allow the Lord to fill in the blanks.

The other way of knowing what needs prayer is to be familiar, to the extent possible, with the history of the home or property. Go as far back as you can through research. Who originally owned the land? Was it part of a broken treaty with Native Americans? Who has owned it since, and what is their reputation? Has any illegal activity ever been recorded there? A trip to your local library and talking to a few neighbors often reveal some very pertinent information. Remember, it does not matter if you own a home or if you rent an apartment. If you have a legal right to inhabit a place, then you have the spiritual authority to pray cleansing over that place.

Praying over Land

When you get an idea about any sin that may have given the enemy a foothold in your home, the first step is to pray a prayer of repentance, like Joan did for Joey's situation. Even though you may not have been the one who committed the sin, you can go to God on behalf of whoever committed the sin and ask Him to forgive that sin and apply the blood of Jesus to the land. This is called identificational repentance.

Doing this does not mean that people who actually commit sin will not have to answer to God for their actions. They will. What identificational repentance does, however, is bring the blood of Jesus into the situation in order to cut off the sin's ongoing effects. It shuts the door to demonic occupancy in that place. Any demonic force that has been there because of a particular sin issue can, at that point, be commanded to leave in Jesus' name. They must do so because their legal right (which was linked with unremitted sin) has been removed. We can then pray and invite the Holy Spirit into the land and dedicate it for God's use. By doing these things, we actually have the power to bring cleansing to land that has been defiled and protect our homes from spiritual darkness.

we can pray and invite the Holy spirit into the land and dedicate it for god's use.

Sometimes it is good to *stake your land*. In other words, go to the boundaries of your land, take Communion and declare to the powers and principalities that you are now in authority over that land. Many people write on stakes Scripture verses that are very dear to their hearts and actually drive the stakes into the corner intersection points of their land. Therefore, the Word of God forms the boundary of that land. You then have the legal right and authority to declare the manifold wisdom of God to any evil force that crosses those boundaries.

Returning to the Land

The actual land can grieve once a sin is committed upon the ground. Because of this, once we are filled with the Spirit of God, He may require us to return and stand upon the place where the defilement occurred. One of the hardest things I had to do was to return to a place in Galveston, Texas, where my family fell apart. The wound and trauma in that particular place was linked deep to the emotions of my soul. The only way my emotions could be cleansed was for me to go back and stand on the place where the trauma actually occurred. The first time I attempted to do this, I was overwhelmed with sickness. Many of our infirmities are linked with trauma.

My mother, my sister and I had gone down to visit my dad who was working and overseeing a project offshore in the Gulf of Mexico. While we were there, a terrible situation occurred that became violent. This was one of the defining times of my life. The domestic violence situation was so intense that I wondered if we would escape alive. We were staying in a hotel room when this occurred. Years later the Lord made me revisit the hotel room in order to break the defilement of the situation. I was spiritually mature enough the second time I attempted to do this.

I stood there with my wife and thanked God for our wonderful relationship in the actual hotel room where the horrible situation had occurred 25 years earlier. I then asked forgiveness for my bloodline, which had produced such a horrid atmosphere in that hotel room. I asked forgiveness for the blood that was shed there. I asked the Lord to heal the trauma in my heart and emotions, as well as the land I was standing on. I asked the Lord to disconnect the spirit of infirmity that was linked to the trauma of that situation. As a result, God was faithful to cleanse the land and produce a new level of healing in my life.

Staying in Hotel Rooms

An interesting side note to the discussion of defiled land is hotel rooms. A great deal of immorality and who knows what else takes place in hotels—many times in the very rooms in which we stay and on the beds in which we sleep. Many good Christians have been inadvertently exposed to pornography through the television or through magazines left by others. Such things can hook otherwise innocent people into a lasting sin problem. How can we protect ourselves from a cheap shot by the enemy when we're on the road?

A simple prayer can expel the demons and keep them from attacking us.

When we rent a room for a period of time, we have legal spiritual authority over the atmosphere while we are there. A simple prayer can expel the demons and keep them from attacking us while we occupy that room. Whenever you enter a hotel room, stop and pray, asking God to forgive any sins of abuse, idolatry, bloodshed, immorality, covenant breaking, occult activity or whatever else may be impressing you at the time. Then pray a prayer binding any forces linked with those sins from operating while you are there.

Also pay special attention to the artwork and pictures. If anything looks strange, unnatural or demonic, pray cleansing from evil spirits, and pray that any curses attached to those objects would be broken. Taking the time to pray this way can make a tremendous difference in your trip!

Walking the Land

The Lord told Joshua: "Every place that the sole of your foot will tread upon I have given you" (Josh. 1:3). From the soles of our feet, we emit life or death, very much like our tongues. If the glory of God permeates through our bodies, then wherever we walk experiences that glory and light. Light dispels darkness. Therefore, if we are filled with light, then wherever we walk darkness has to flee. When trauma has occurred on a piece of property or land and we are walking on that land, we bring change. Either we will discern where the trauma is and ask God how to bring healing, or else we will have authority to heal the land. The earth and the fullness thereof is the Lord's. We are representatives in causing the earth to reflect the fullness of God's plan:

> Then the LORD will be zealous for His land, and pity His people. The LORD will answer and say to His people, "Behold, I will send you grain and new wine and oil, and you will be satisfied by them; I will no longer make you a reproach among the nations." Fear not, O land; be glad and rejoice, for the LORD has done marvelous things! Do not be afraid, you beasts of the field; for the open pastures are springing up, and the tree bears its fruit; the fig tree and the vine yield their strength (Joel 2:18-19,21-22).

This is such an incredible promise! It is given in the midst of a call to repentance. Once there has been defilement, if we change our minds and operate in the opposite spirit upon the land that was defiled, we will see the land become fruitful.

Your land can rejoice!

Notes

1. *The American Heritage Dictionary of the English Language,* 4th ed., s.v. "foothold."
2. Other entry points for demonization include victimization, rejection, trauma, witchcraft, occult, fraternal orders (including Freemasonry) and cursing. An excellent study on this topic as it relates to issues of land is Bob Beckett's *Commitment to Conquer* (Grand Rapids, MI: Chosen Books, 1997).
3. *The American Heritage Dictionary of the English Language,* 4th ed., s.v. "topographical."

Overthrowing Generational Curses

With the day's business behind me, I decided to take a walk and explore New Orleans. As I ventured out of my hotel, I took in the sights of a place where the excitement never seemed to end. Crowds of visitors, tourists and locals lined both sides of Bourbon Street as they streamed in and out of shops, bars, restaurants and establishments that offered live sex shows. Small groups gathered around jazz bands, many dancing to the music. I heard an occasional roar of laughter, along with an argument in what sounded like French.

As I walked along taking in all of the activity, I found myself stopping in front of one particular shop. In the window was a beautiful ceramic cat with riveting blue eyes. The noise of the street seemed to fade as my concentration turned to the cat. I seemed drawn to it. I decided to take a closer look. The shop was filled with oddities, many of which were used in voodoo rituals. I thought little of it as I picked up the ceramic cat and gave it a closer inspection. Even though it was quite expensive, I had to have it. This beautiful cat would look great by the fireplace.

Generational Influences

In chapter 4, I tell the rest of the story of this ceramic cat. One day the Lord revealed to me that witchcraft was linked to the cat. After all, it was purchased in a shop with voodoo items. I should have known better, but at the time I was ignorant of the principles outlined in this book. Even so, many Christians would have shied away from the shop based on the weird feel of the place alone. I did not. In fact, I felt drawn to the shop. Why? Because of generational influences in my bloodline.

Occult practices were not unusual in previous generations of my family. I had seen occult power at work. I remember one instance in particular when my grandfather and I were working and we encountered a wasps' nest in the middle of a doorway we were trying to get through. He looked at his palm, spoke something to it and held it up, resulting in every one of the wasps dropping dead right before our eyes. He had used occult power to kill the wasps!

How is it that the actions of my grandfather and others in my ancestry had anything to do with my entering a questionable shop years later? Because I had inherited a weakness toward sins of occult and witchcraft that had been passed down through my family's bloodline. That weakness, known as iniquity, was operating in my life when I visited New Orleans and bought the cat. How can this be? Exodus 20:5 offers the answer: "For I, the LORD your God, am a jealous God, visiting the iniquity of the fathers upon the children to the third and fourth generations." Sin not only affects the land (see chapter 5), but it also affects bloodlines for generations.

In *The Voice of God*, Cindy Jacobs helps us understand sin and iniquity as it relates to the generations:

> The Bible speaks of them as two different things. Sin is basically the cause, and iniquity includes the effect. Generational iniquity works like this: A parent can commit a sin such as occultic involvement or sexual sin and that produces a curse. The curse then causes a generational iniquity or weakness to pass down in the family line.
>
> Here is an example that might clarify this process. A pregnant woman is x-rayed and the unborn child becomes deformed by the X ray. The unborn child didn't order the X ray and is entirely a victim but, nonetheless, is affected by the X ray. Sin, like the X ray, damages the generations. This is an awesome thought and should put the fear of the Lord in us before we enter into sin.[1]

Iniquitous Patterns

Have you ever noticed how, for example, alcoholism, divorce, laziness or greed tends to run in families? These aren't just learned behaviors. They are manifestations of iniquity that have been passed down in the generations—in other words, iniquitous patterns. Of course, there are isolated instances of sin that seem to have nothing to do with previous generations. In that case, a new iniquitous pattern may be beginning in a family if that sin is not made right before God. If you start looking around you with this in mind, you may be surprised at how many iniquitous patterns of sin you can find in family lines.[2]

Familial Spirits

Through the sin and iniquitous pattern, a familial spirit controls a certain person in a family. Sin is an opening for demonic forces to work in subsequent generations of a family through

sin is an opening for demonic forces to work in subsequent generations.

the iniquity produced. They know the family weaknesses and, therefore, entice, tempt or lure family members with that weakness into the same or related sin. Spirits that are assigned to a family are called familial spirits. Some have been in families for generations on end.[3]

Generational Curses

"Curse" is defined as the cause of evil, misfortune or trouble.[4] John Eckhardt of Crusaders Ministries defines it this way:

> A curse is God's recompense in the life of a person and his or her descendants as a result of iniquity. The curse causes sorrow of heart and gives demonic spirits legal entry into a family whereby they can carry out and perpetuate their wicked devices.[5]

Eckhardt goes on to quote Derek Prince's seven common indications of a curse: chronic financial problems, chronic sickness and disease, female problems (I would add barrenness, whether brought on by the husband or the wife), prone to have accidents, marital problems, premature death and mental illness. Eckhardt adds mistreatment and abuse by others, and wandering or vagabond tendencies to the list.[6]

Such curses are produced because of the law of reaping and sowing. When a particular sin takes hold in the generations, a family curse is part of the effects of that sin.[7]

Generational Sin and Iniquity Susceptibility

There are certain things we can see in our family history that can help us identify what problems may be affecting us today. In *The Voice of God*, Cindy Jacobs identifies four things that make us particularly susceptible to generational sin and iniquity:

1. Occultic Involvement and Witchcraft. Anything that draws its power from a source other than God is demonic in nature and can produce problems in the generations.

2. Secret Societies. This category includes Freemasonry, Eastern Star and the Shriners. Members are often required to take oaths that actually curse themselves and their families.[8] If you or an ancestor has been involved in Freemasonry, see appendix A of this book.

3. Robbing and Defrauding God. If you withhold your tithe (10 percent) from God, the Bible says that you are actually robbing Him and that a curse can come into your household as a result (see Mal. 3:8-9). This curse often manifests itself as financial trouble, including poverty, and can be passed from generation to generation.

4. Bondages. Bondages are often passed down through family lines. Dean Sherman defines "bondages" this way: "If we continue in a habit of sin, we can develop a bondage. Bondage means that there is a supernatural element to our problem. The enemy now has a grip on a function of our personality."[9]

The Problem of Objects

What do these generational influences have to do with protecting your home from spiritual darkness? As we discussed in chapter 3, objects that you own can often represent demonic strongholds in your life. They also can represent iniquitous patterns or generational curses, and they may be the hiding place for familial spirits. That was the case with my ceramic cat. It represented a weakness in my family of being drawn to things linked with the occult (as we explained in chapter 3, ceramic cats in general are not linked with demonic forces, but this particular one was). Ask the Lord to begin to show you what generational iniquities run in your family and what objects you own that might be linked with those iniquities.

The Problem of Heirlooms

Does everything passed down to you from a grandparent have to go? Of course not! The issue is determining what items are linked with iniquitous patterns, generational curses or ungodliness and then removing those objects from your home. It may be helpful to review the list of suspect objects in chapter 3.

Getting rid of something you have purchased is one thing, but destroying something that has been passed on to you may be another matter. Many people are often unwilling to give up something that may have belonged to an ancestor, either out of a sense of sentimentality or family pride, or a need to honor the ancestor, which is especially prevalent in Asian cultures that believe in spiritism.

Spiritism is communicating with demonic forces that are linked with the dead. Spiritualism is the belief that the dead survive as spirits and can communicate with the living. Many people hold on to an object because they feel it links them with someone who has died. In that case, the object has become more than a memento of a loved one. It has become a means of keeping spiritual contact with the dead person. In reality, the heirloom is not maintaining a link to their dead loved one but rather to a familial spirit who enjoys access to their homes through deception.

what dark forces are we allowing into our homes by owning certain heirlooms?

We must ask ourselves what dark forces we may be allowing into our homes by owning certain heirlooms. Do those objects honor God? Do they keep us in bondage to a generational curse or familial spirit? Can we reach the destiny God has for us while continuing to allow openings to the demonic in our own homes? What effect do those objects have on our children? Do we have a greater responsibility to honor past generations or to mold new ones? Some things may be difficult to let go of, but we must honestly measure what we own against these kinds of questions, not only in our own minds, but also prayerfully before God.

If you remain unconvinced or have further questions about the cause and effect of generational sin and iniquity, you may want to read our book *Possessing Your Inheritance* (Regal Books, 1999), which offers an in-depth treatment of the subject.

A Locket with Hair

Our family has a friend named Penny Jackson who lives in Houston. She had decided to come up for a weekend visit. Knowing that our church has a deliverance ministry, she had chosen to use this time to also pursue and review any spiritual issues in her life that could hinder her future. Here is Penny's testimony of her deliverance:

> Recently before I was planning to go in for a ministry time in Denton, I was filling out the questionnaire that asked about family ties, past dabbling in the occult, and so on. As I filled out the questionnaire, the Lord strongly quickened to me a piece of jewelry that my father had gotten for me years ago—in fact, 30 or more years ago. My father knew I loved antique jewelry and had given me an opal ring from an antique shop in downtown Dallas. Probably a man's pinky ring, it had a beautiful opal in the middle surrounded by black enamel. On the inside of the ring was inscribed March 25. I had felt prompted to get rid of this ring after hearing a specific teaching concerning objects. (I can't even remember now what the teaching was.)
>
> The other piece of jewelry he gave me was a locket from that same shop. This gold locket was engraved with flowery designs and birds on the front as well as some initials. What stood out to me, though, was that this locket had "A birthday present, March 25/60" engraved in it as well as a lock of hair preserved under a piece of heavy glass. Because this store dealt with antiques from England in the 1800s, the consensus was that the "/60" was 1860.
>
> Not knowing then what I do now about spiritual things, I thought that March 25 must surely be a special

date to me. The fact that I caught a bridal bouquet soon after that at a March 25 wedding did nothing to change my opinion. Fortunately as years passed, I learned more about the things of the Spirit and realized that "lucky days" didn't have a place where the Lord was concerned. I repented for that mind-set.

I really haven't worn the locket much or even given it much thought until this night recently when it was so clearly brought to my attention by the Lord. When I located the locket and picked it up, a strange feeling came all over me. I felt the Lord was clearly leading me to deal with this object. So I packed it up to come to the ministry appointment. When I showed it to Chuck, he immediately felt what I had felt when I picked it up. It was just creepy. I don't know how else to say it.

When I went to the ministry time, I brought the locket. We placed it on the table but didn't do anything with it right away. The two women ministering to me felt something strange about it also. I had felt the night before that I wanted to break it open and see if there was anything behind the fabric the lock of hair lay on. When we finally got it open and I took the hair out with tweezers, there was just the most powerful presence that invaded the room. There was nothing behind the lock of hair, but the hair itself brought a strong supernatural feeling—so bad, in fact, that we had to take it totally out of the church building.

Chuck reminded me of the significance of hair. Hair contains the DNA of an individual. Many times in witchcraft or magic rituals, people place a curse upon hair and then plant that hair on the person of the individual being cursed. One of the women felt that there was a curse linked with an inordinate affection that had been placed upon the locket. Regardless of what all it meant, we knew that the hair certainly was not of God.

There is some reason why my father was drawn to those two pieces of jewelry. He didn't even know, if memory serves, that the two had the same dates on them. Those in the deliverance session discussed how this type of knowledge about an object could cause a certain course of action to be set in the spiritual realm. Chuck suggested that I hang on to the locket until I had heard everything the Lord had to say about it. The locket definitely felt better since the hair was gone—not great, but better. When I returned to Houston, I began to do research on the date March 25. I checked family records and could find no instances of March 25. I then went to the Internet where I found that March 25 is a day called Lady Day that used to be when Christmas was celebrated until it was moved to December. However, March 25 remained a day that some goddess worshipers celebrated because it was nine months before the birth of Christ and, therefore, conception day. And it was a time of spring when pagan cultures worshiped because of the return of spring, also goddess-related, I believe. So this was a date and time period that had spiritual significance. There was also a pagan rite, which occurred in March in which a representative couple had sexual intercourse while others looked on and celebrated to represent the sacred union between the male and female and their equal importance in religion.

I am still asking God about this piece of jewelry. I feel at the right time when a full revelation comes to me, I will then remove this from being a part of my life. And the cycle of whatever this ring represents will be broken and a new dimension of destiny will be released for me.[10]

After reading this chapter, the Lord may open your eyes to many objects that need to be dealt with in your home. Just as Penny took her time with this one object, take your time. Let God reveal to you the real issue behind the object He has put His finger on. Only deal with what God is dealing with in your life and home. The Lord Jesus Christ has already paid the price for your total freedom. Take your time and allow the redemptive plan He has for you to fully mature.

Notes
1. Cindy Jacobs, *The Voice of God* (Ventura, CA: Regal Books, 1995), p. 64.
2. Chuck D. Pierce and Rebecca Wagner Sytsema, *Possessing Your Inheritance* (Ventura, CA: Regal Books, 1999), pp. 172-173.
3. Ibid., p. 174.
4. *The American Heritage Dictionary of the English Language,* 4th ed., s.v. "curse."
5. John Eckhardt, *Identifying and Breaking Curses* (Chicago: Crusaders Ministries, 1995), p. 1.
6. Ibid., p. 10.
7. Pierce and Sytsema, *Possessing Your Inheritance,* pp. 175-176.
8. For further study on Freemasonry, we recommend reading chapter 10 of Noel and Phyl Gibson's *Evicting Demonic Intruders* (West Sussex, England: New Wine Press, 1993).
9. Dean Sherman, *Spiritual Warfare for Every Christian* (Seattle, WA: Frontline Communications, 1990), p. 107; Cindy Jacobs, *The Voice of God* (Ventura, CA: Regal Books, 1995), pp. 65-67.
10. Penny Jackson, e-mail message to Chuck Pierce, April 19, 2004.

CHAPTER SEVEN

PROTECTING OUR CHILDREN FROM SPIRITUAL DARKNESS

He who fears the LORD has a secure fortress, and for his children it will be a refuge.
PROVERBS 14:26, *NIV*

We have looked at many issues that allow spiritual darkness into a home. The goal of this chapter is to help parents understand some issues that are specific to their children. Securing your children's spiritual freedom is an important step to protecting your home from spiritual darkness.

The Importance of Order

Now that we have briefly discussed generational sin, let's look at God's order in the family, primarily focusing on children.

In *The Christian Family*, Larry Christenson writes:

> The secret of good family life is disarmingly simple: *cultivate the family's relationship with Jesus Christ*. There is no phase of family life left outside this relationship. There is no problem a family might face which does not find its solution within the scope of this objective.[1]

The most important way to cultivate your family's relationship with the Lord is to establish God's divine order in your home. God's divine order has to do with relationship and authority.

In both the Old Testament and New Testament, we find one key statement for children's relationships, which is to obey their parents, for this is pleasing to the Lord and will create long life for them (see Exod. 20:12; Col. 3:20). A child's relationship to the Father, Jesus and the Holy Spirit usually thrives and prospers in direct proportion to his or her obedience in the home and to his or her parents. If you can teach your children obedience as prescribed in Hebrews 12, they will not only become children filled with joy and freedom, but they also will mature into adults filled with faith.

The word "order" means to command or give orders in sequence to produce a specific result. "Order" also means the arrangement of position and rank, resulting in the ultimate accomplishment so that peace occurs in one's person or environment.[2] The word, therefore, includes both relationship and authority—the very things we need to cultivate the family's relationship to Jesus Christ. Order also brings boundaries. I believe the real key for children's lives is to show them the boundaries that have been established for their prosperity. These boundaries include being aware that owning certain things could give place to the enemy who longs to steal their peace and prosperity from an early age. Therefore, it is very important that we teach children to remove anything that enters their boundaries that would cause their peace to be lost or their prosperity to dwindle.

God's purpose is for us to be whole. The quicker we can teach this to our children, the better off they will be. First Thessalonians 5:23 reads: "Now may the God of peace Himself sanctify you completely; and may your whole spirit, soul, and body be preserved blameless at the coming of our Lord Jesus Christ." I believe this should be every parent's goal for his or her child.

Generational Issues in a Child's Life

With the basis we established for generational issues in chapter 6, let's take another look at those issues in relationship to the order of a child's life. Because a generational iniquity can be passed from generation to generation to generation (see Exod. 20:5), I believe it is important to look for the patterns of generational iniquity in a child's life.

We can do this by observing a child's outward actions and by watching what kinds of items draw the child's attention. One key symptom is if a child forms an addiction at an early age. Sometimes children's appetites are totally out of control. Sometimes they show signs of behavioral extremes and compulsive patterns. Often parents have been delivered totally of generational curses after a similar pattern began appearing in their children. For instance, a parent might be a deceitful person, but through the blood of Jesus and spiritual discipline, the parent overcomes the problem in his or her own life only to find that his or her child still becomes deceitful. Any time we overcome a generational iniquity, it weakens that iniquitous pattern in the bloodline. I believe sometimes we can do away with it, but sometimes it appears in a weakened form.

> often parents have been delivered of generational curses after a similar pattern began appearing in their children.

My wife, Pam, and I have five children. Pam and I had difficult childhoods that were mixed with both good and evil inheritances from the generations. Even though we have broken many generational iniquities and curses in our own lives, I do not assume the patterns have been annihilated completely. We always watch our children for signs of recurring patterns of what we know existed in the generations before us.

This principle appears throughout the Word of God. When Joshua, for instance, entered into the Promised Land, he defeated many but not all of the enemies. Some still remained in the land. Then we see David, four generations later, ridding the land of the Jebusites. We need to be aware of this principle in light of our children.

Sharing Experiences from the Children's Home

In the early 1980s, Pam and I had the privilege of becoming the administrators of one of the largest children's homes in Texas. This home was for children from broken families. Many of the kids were on the verge of becoming juvenile delinquents because the order of their lives had become so disrupted through a dysfunctional family unit. We learned many valuable lessons concerning the restoration of a child's innocence, resulting in a reestablishment of his or her future. I believe that sharing some of these experiences will help you better detect demonic behavior in children.

One 13-year-old boy whom we loved dearly and were responsible for had real problems with pornography and sexual addiction. His problem went far beyond any normal sexual curiosity. We had authority over the cottage he lived in, as well as when he came into our personal home. Therefore, we knew that God had given us authority and influence to restore the godly order of his life.

We set boundaries over this child. We explained the evils of pornography to him. Whenever he stayed within those boundaries, he was fine. However, every time he got out from under our authority, he fell into the same patterns of sin—gaining access to pornographic materials. Pam and I began to cry out to God for his deliverance. We needed to find the entry point in his life that gave this demonic force the right to influence him and keep him bound with pornographic materials.

We eventually learned that he was conceived out of wedlock and was born into a perverted situation. The environment he lived in was fatherless, and the male figures that came into his life had only presented a perverse example of masculinity. These facts helped us pray for his deliverance with great success. He is now a young man with a family who remains delivered to this day. The point is that sometimes we need to see how the objects to which our children are drawn are linked with iniquitous patterns in their bloodline.

sometimes we need to see how the objects to which our children are drawn are linked with iniquitous patterns in their bloodline.

Infiltrating Boundaries

As was the case with this boy, it is important that we know how demons enter so that we can gain authority over their eviction. Consider, for example, the story about the woman with the spirit of infirmity that caused her back to be bent over (see Luke 13:10-13). The Bible says she had been bound for 18 years, which means prior to that she had been free and at some point Satan afflicted her. You can always look back to the time when there was freedom to see where the enemy gained access. If there never has been freedom, we have authority through Jesus to establish it now.

I believe that every generation should excel beyond the one before. I want my children to establish a greater glory within their boundaries than I have. However, I also know that the enemy wants to infiltrate their boundaries and not only bring them into captivity but also cause the ground we have gained to be lost. Because this is the case, I always want to be protective of the order in my children's lives until they have fully established God's authority for themselves. I always review my children's boundaries and the order of their lives by the following:

1. The Generational Bloodline.

2. Their Own Personal Sin. Remember, kids are kids—they are born degenerate and with free will. I, of course, try to steer them away from sinning. Yet whenever I see my children choosing to sin, I look for the consequences of that sin in their lives. Then I explain why they are suffering those consequences so that they can develop within them a hatred of that sin.

3. Occultic Activity. I look for any power of occult that has an influence in my children's lives. The word "occult" simply means hidden.[3] I find that Satan tries to create deception and hide the truth of sin to a child. My job is to expose sin for what it is.

4. Roots of Bitterness and Unforgiveness. One of the children for whom Pam and I were responsible in the children's home had tremendous potential. I believe every child has potential, but this child was unique. However, he had been flunking school and had been truant for two months. He had big problems. The Lord often revealed to me what this boy had in his possession. Sometimes it was drugs, other times it was weapons. He was eventually caught at school with drugs; and when I told him of the punishment the authorities at school set for him, he rebelled violently.

The Lord showed me a root of hate and murder within him. He had been a part of a very good family that had fallen apart because of his dad's infidelity. The bitterness from the loss was very deeply rooted. I remember the night that the root of bitterness was finally dealt with. When that occurred, he immediately accepted the Lord as his Savior and his life and countenance changed suddenly and dramatically. He brought many, many things to me that represented his past nature and the bitterness that had been in him.

Dealing with a Younger Child

When dealing with younger children, demonic forces often torment them through fear. In their excellent book *A Manual for Children's Deliverance*, Frank and Ida Mae Hammond say, "Night troublers are common: fear of the dark, fear of being left alone, or fear 'something is going to get you.' We have found such fears rooted in television programs, terrifying experiences, abusive treatment, and in toys and objects in the child's bedroom."[4]

When a child exhibits fear of something in his or her room, trace the fear to the source. It may be as simple as a shadow cast by a stuffed animal. In this case, eliminate the shadow by moving the toy. At other times, the fear may be there as a result of some hidden item that needs to be uncovered. Enlist the child's assistance. Spend time "talking out" his or her fears. Because a child is more aware of what bothers him or her than we are, the child can often pinpoint the item. Allow the child to sift through his or her toys, games, music, pictures and books to show you what is bothersome.

However, children cannot always determine the source of their problems, and that's where they need your help. Here is a list of some items to watch for:

1. Video games with occult or martial arts themes
2. Posters or pictures with occult or frightening images
3. Books with scary pictures inside or on the cover
4. Books of an occult or questionable origin
5. Toys or other items of a frightening or occult nature[5]

Caution: Many parents worry about their children's imaginations. There is a difference between creative, God-given imagination and occult fantasies. I have seen many parents harm the development of their children's godly imaginations and creativity by "throwing out the baby with the bath water." Do not become legalistic with your child. This only causes the creativity of God not to manifest in the child. Many times this also results in a poverty mentality.

You can learn the difference by seeing how your child's imagination is affecting his or her behavior. Is your child obsessed by his or her fantasies? Are the fantasies rooted in violence or anger? Here is where we can all use some parental common sense. As you deal with your child, remember that the forming of a child's conscience is important. You want to instill moral character, but not religious legalism. I have found it best to present my children with the right choice, instead of forcing a choice upon them.

As for teaching a child about spiritual discernment, here is some good advice from Graham and Shirley Powell:

> Children can easily grasp the realities of spiritual conflict, and should be taught how they can do their part to keep themselves walking closely with Jesus. But it is imperative that these truths be shared in wisdom so that there is no ground given for fear of the enemy. The reality of Jesus being Lord and Satan being defeated must be imparted. Continually center their attention on the love, power, and glory of the Lord Jesus Christ. Let them grow up Christ-conscious.[6]

Extending Boundaries

As children become older and more mature, parents have to extend boundaries. Every time you extend boundaries, you have to allow the child to establish new authority and responsibility within his or her new boundaries. You, therefore, have to watch for what new influences come into the child's life. This can be very difficult for parents who would like their children to remain innocent and do not train them to discern the evils they will encounter.

Music is a great example. One of our sons went to the movie *Godzilla* and used his own money to buy the soundtrack. About a week later, I just happened to be talking to him about the movie (which I would not have gone to see to start with) as he was playing the soundtrack. I heard a song that I thought was terrible, so I tried to approach him to discuss the song and look at the words together. He resisted, so I asked the Lord to show him. A few nights later, he was visited by an evil, tangible presence. The force was the same color as that on the soundtrack. Because of the color, he knew that the evil presence was linked with the soundtrack he had bought. He immediately confessed the sin to his mother and me and destroyed the CD. With that act of obedience, the evil presence left. Even though he still experiments with some music, he now understands that evil power can reside in it and exercises a level of discernment he did not previously exhibit.

The Magic 8 Ball

My son Isaac once took his allowance and bought what is known as the Magic 8 Ball. This is an object that you ask a question to, shake it and then an answer pops up in the eye of the ball. It is just another form of the evil eye that seduces children.

I went into his room and began telling him that he had purchased an occult object. Of course, he retorted, "Dad, you think everything is evil!" I asked the Lord how to handle the situation. I left the room and prayed that Isaac would see the demonic force behind this object. Within a couple of days, an unknown fear began to grab hold of him. With our older children, he had watched part of a movie that had really affected him. However, the fear he was experiencing was beyond anything that was natural. His sister asked forgiveness for allowing him to watch part of the movie. He asked forgiveness for watching it.

Yet his fear continued. He told me that he felt like something was watching him in the middle of the night. I knew it was that eight ball. However, I was waiting for God to deal with him over this issue. Three days later, he came to me with a totally different attitude. He asked me to destroy the eight ball with him, which I did. He slept fine that night.

Hidden Things Revealed

As children grow older, they may become involved in activities that they choose to hide from their parents. The Holy Spirit, however, has the power to reveal hidden things to parents. This was another lesson I learned while working at the children's home. There was one particular boy who reminded me of Eddie Haskell on *Leave It to Beaver*. He could be real sweet, but he had a side we needed to watch out for.

The Holy Spirit can reveal hidden things that may cause danger for your children.

Once a month, the kids had the choice to go back and visit whatever home life they came from. These visits often caused a lot of problems, because they got away from the influence of a godly environment and were immersed in situations that caused their troubles in the first place. One weekend, our "Eddie Haskell" decided to go home. Pam and I went to church that Sunday as usual. During the service, there was an altar call. When I went up to the altar, the Lord revealed to me that our

Eddie was coming back with a duffel bag. The Lord also showed me everything inside this bag.

When the boy returned that afternoon, I explained to him what the Lord showed me at the altar. I then listed everything inside his duffel bag including rock music, snuff and marijuana. Our Eddie turned white as a sheet. I was right on every count. He quickly repented. But more important, he saw the power of God to reveal the unknown.

The Holy Spirit can reveal hidden things that may cause danger for your children. This is sometimes necessary when raising children. Therefore, listen and respond to the Holy Spirit.

In Closing

Raising kids is one of the more difficult assignments in a world today filled with enticing, seducing forces. I wish we had more insight and a 1-2-3 method to help you. However, one thing we have learned with our children is not to major on minors. Many times we can get so caught up in wanting everything to be perfect that we miss the overall issue of what God is trying to do in a child. Children must be molded. They also must experiment. Therefore, in the midst of their maturing and experimenting, we must find creative ways to discipline and mold them.

It is important that we as parents have a heart to see our children's wholeness. We must help them understand the order that God has established for their lives. We must make them aware that God wants them to prosper within the boundaries He has established for them. We must show them how to detect for themselves when anything detrimental enters or disrupts God's order in their lives. We must trust God daily to rid our children's lives of spiritual darkness.

Let me caution you not to provoke your children. Talk to them. Let them help set boundaries. Let them explain to you why they are doing certain things. In the same way, express your heart and conscience to them, and let them know that you have set certain limitations on their freedom as long as they live within your home. Never let the devil create a situation that cuts off your communication. Find creative ways to communicate with your children and include them in decisions that affect them personally, as well as the whole family.

Let me end with this simple story. When Rebekah, our only daughter, was a child she came to me and asked me to watch a movie with her. I resisted and protested at first. The movie was Disney's *The Little Mermaid*. I knew about the story and really saw all sorts of issues, because there was a witch in the movie and so on and so on. However, I felt the Holy Spirit check me. When we sat down and together watched the movie about this rebellious mermaid who went against everything her father said, something very interesting happened. My daughter began to weep and say, "Dad, I never want to be like that toward you." The Lord used this movie greatly in our lives.

The real issue in God's heart is that fathers' hearts turn toward their children, and children's hearts turn toward their fathers, so that no curse can come in and wreak havoc against God's destined plan in our generations.

Notes

1. Larry Christenson, *The Christian Family* (Minneapolis, MN: Bethany House Publishing, 1970), p. 15.
2. *The American Heritage Dictionary of the English Language*, 4th ed., s.v. "order."
3. Ibid., s.v. "occult."
4. Frank D. and Ida Mae Hammond, *A Manual for Children's Deliverance* (Kirkwood, MO: Impact Christian Books, 1996), p. 81.
5. See *A Manual for Children's Deliverance* for a more complete list of games and toys to watch for.
6. Graham and Shirley Powell, *Christian, Set Yourself Free* (Kent, England: Sovereign World Ltd., 1983), p. 165.

CHAPTER EIGHT

TEN STEPS TO PROTECTING YOUR HOME FROM SPIRITUAL DARKNESS

Now that we have discussed a number of principles you need to know in order to do spiritual housecleaning, let's look at the whole process step-by-step. As you read through this chapter, please remember that this might take some time. Do not try to rush the process along. For instance, you may find that you need more time to do personal repentance than you thought or to look through your house for objects that need to go. Allow the Holy Spirit to set the pace for you.

Also remember that you do not have to own a home or property to follow this list. If you rent a house or apartment, you have the spiritual legal right to evict Satan's cohorts.

Step 1: Accept Jesus as Your Lord and Savior

Most of you probably have already taken this step, but for those of you who have not, the very first step to protecting your home from spiritual darkness is to secure your relationship to God by accepting Jesus as your Lord and Savior. It is through Jesus' name that we have the authority to expel demonic forces, and we cannot avail ourselves of using His name unless we have relationship with Him.

There is something much more important at stake—your eternal home. Living with spiritual darkness on Earth is one thing, but living in utter and complete darkness with no hope of life for all eternity is another. Only the blood of Jesus can save you from such an awful fate. If you have not already secured your salvation, you must turn away from sin, believe in the death and resurrection of Jesus and receive Him as Lord and Savior of your life. To do this you must do the following:

1. Consider your life and then turn away from everything that is contrary to what God wants (see Matt. 3:7-10; Acts 3:19).

2. Acknowledge that Jesus Christ died on the cross to forgive you of sin and that you take Him as your Savior to cleanse you from sin. Jesus paid the price due for your sin (see Rom. 5:9-10; Titus 2:14).

3. Ask Him to be the Lord of your life, acknowledging openly and verbally that Jesus is not only your Savior but also your Lord (see 1 John 2:23).[1]

Step 2: Take a Spiritual Inventory of Your Life

In order to remove demonic forces from our homes and keep them out, we must be willing to deal with sin issues in our lives. As Charles Kraft, professor at Fuller Theological Seminary, would describe it, demons are like rats and sin is like garbage. "If we get rid of the rats and keep the garbage, the person is in great danger still. But if we get rid of the garbage, what we have done automatically affects the rats."[2] In other words, you must get rid of the garbage in order to get rid of the rats.

When we rid our lives of sin, demonic forces do not have the legal right they once had to occupy our lives and our homes. However, if we go through these steps to protect our homes from demonic forces without making our lives right before God, we may actually make our situation worse!

Jesus taught that if we cast out a demon and it does not find rest elsewhere, the demon comes back to check out the situation. If the demon finds the house is still suitable for occupation, then it goes and finds seven other demons—even more wicked than itself—and they all set up shop right back where they started. If we expel one demon but do not remove its legal right, we get eight in return. And our final condition is worse than the first (see Matt. 12:43-45).

Ask the Lord to reveal any sin issues in your life that must be dealt with before continuing in this process. Because unforgiveness is a big bag of garbage on which demons love to feed, ask God to show you any places of unforgiveness toward others that you need to correct.

Step 3: Dedicate Your Home to the Lord

The next step in protecting your home from spiritual darkness is to dedicate it to the Lord. Simply pray and invite the presence of the Lord into your home. Ask the Lord to use your home for His purposes. Declare that as for you and your house, you will serve the Lord (see Josh. 24:15). Declare that your home will not be a haven for dark forces; rather, it will be a beacon of light for your family and to the world. It is best to pray these things in an audible voice, which affirms your intentions not only to God and to yourself but also to any forces of darkness that are about to lose their dwelling place.

Step 4: Prepare for Battle

What we are engaged in is spiritual warfare. We are warring in the heavenlies to establish our homes for the Lord and declare them off limits to the powers of darkness. Here are the preparations we should make as we go into battle:

- Ask the Lord for the strategy of your war. He may lead you to play praise music throughout your home for a period of time, or He may lead you to read specific Scriptures in each room. Expect that He will answer your prayer and show you how to proceed.

· Plead the blood of Jesus over yourself, your family, your animals and your property.
· Pray Psalm 91 out loud.
· In Jesus' name, bind any demonic forces from manifesting in your home during this process.

Step 5: Take a Spiritual Inventory of Your Home

Ask the Lord to give you the discernment you will need as you look at what you own. Go through your home, room by room, and let the Holy Spirit show you any object that should not be in your home. Review the list of problem objects in chapter 3. Examine your heirlooms as outlined in chapter 6.

Step 6: Cleanse Your Home of Ungodly Objects

Whatever needs to go should not be considered an item for your next garage sale! Once you know something must go, be careful to destroy it. Deuteronomy 7:25 provides us an example to follow:

You shall burn the carved images of their gods with fire; you shall not covet the silver or gold that is on them, nor take it for yourselves, lest you be snared by it; for it is an abomination to the LORD your God.

Take what can be burned and burn it. If it cannot be burned, pass it through the fire (as a symbolic act of obedience) and then destroy it by whatever other means are available to you, such as smashing or even flushing. (I have known people to do this with jewelry that cannot be destroyed in other ways.)

Once you have destroyed the object, renounce any participation you or your family have had with that object (whether knowingly or unknowingly) and ask the Lord to forgive you. If the object is linked with Freemasonry, Eastern Star, Job's Daughters, Rainbow for Girls or DeMolay, pray the prayer of release for Freemasons and their descendants (see appendix A).

Because the legal right for demonic forces linked with that object have been removed through these acts, you can now command any demonic forces linked with that object to leave in the name of Jesus.

Repeat these steps for every object that needs to go.

Step 7: Cleanse Each Room and Cleanse the Land

After cleansing your home of ungodly objects, the next step is to cleanse the spiritual atmosphere of each room. Demonic forces not attached to an object but in the home because of sin or trauma that occurred there need to be dealt with. Go through each room in your house and repent for any known sin that has been committed.

If someone else occupied your home before you, ask the Lord to show you what needs to be prayed for in each room. Trust the impressions you get during this process. Also, if you have noticed a major change in behavior or circumstances since moving into your home that cannot be explained any other way (e.g., fighting, financial troubles, violence, nightmares, accidents), this might serve as a clue as to what went on in your home before you moved in. Do identificational repentance in each room and over the land (see chapter 5).

Ask the Lord to restore to you and your family whatever blessings were stolen by the enemy through demonic forces in your home.

Pray that the Lord would heal any trauma from the torment of demonic forces in your home. For instance, in chapter 5 we told the story of a three-year-old boy who had been plagued with nightmares of child abuse. In a case like that, you should ask the Lord to touch the boy's mind with His healing balm so that he does not suffer lingering effects of the demonically induced nightmares.

Also, ask the Lord to restore to you and your family whatever blessings were stolen by the enemy through demonic forces in your home.

Step 8: Consecrate Your Home and Your Property

Once you have completed the first seven steps, now it is time to go through your home, room by room, and consecrate each one to the Lord. Speak specific blessings into each room. In the living room, for example, you may want to bless the time that your family spends together and ask the Lord to strengthen those relationships. In each bedroom, bless the plans and purposes that God has for each family member who occupies that room. In the bedroom of a married couple, bless the sexual relationship and the union between husband and wife. Bless the work that goes on in an office or den and declare that all work done will be done as unto the Lord. Think of why each room was designed and then bless that purpose. You can even bless the cleansing that goes on in the bathroom and ask the Lord to use it as a reminder of the cleansing He has brought in your own life!

Many people who consecrate their home room by room use oil to anoint the doors, windows and furnishings. Oil is used as a symbol of Jesus' blood—a reminder of both the cleansing and protecting power in His blood. If you feel so led, use oil. It is certainly appropriate for this type of praying.

Now take a moment to review chapter 5. Once you have completed the process outlined in that chapter, you can consecrate the land to the Lord. One way of doing this is to walk your property's perimeters and declare that the land is consecrated, or set apart, for the Lord. This physical act helps to establish spiritual perimeters.

Another popular way to consecrate land is to stake the land and raise a canopy of praise. Do this by taking wooden stakes and driving one stake in each corner of the property while praying for the Lord's blessing. Then from the center of the property, raise an imaginary canopy of praise to God by worshiping Him, singing songs and declaring Scriptures. Neither of these methods (whether used together or individually) is a magic formula, but rather a symbolic or "prophetic" act that declares to the Lord, to the powers of darkness and to yourself that this property is set apart (i.e., consecrated) for the Lord.

When I moved my family from Denton, Texas, to Colorado Springs, Colorado, we had a housewarming, consecration party in our new home. Along with about 30 friends, we took four oak stakes (about two inches thick) and with a heavy black marker wrote Scripture references on each stake, one on each side of each stake. We used Scriptures such as Psalm 91, Isaiah 54:2-3, Jeremiah 29:7, Luke 1:37 and Joshua 24:15. Teams of about four or five then went to each corner of the property, read the Scriptures listed on their stakes, prayed a prayer of blessing and consecration, and then drove their stake into the ground using a sledgehammer. We then met back in the house and began raising a canopy of praise by worshiping the Lord together.

If you choose to drive stakes into your property, ask the Lord what Scriptures you should use to consecrate the property to Him. You may come up with a whole different list than I did. You don't necessarily need to throw a party either. Do whatever is right for you and your situation.[3]

You can be as creative as you want in finding ways to consecrate your property. I have had friends who placed Bibles in the concrete foundation of the homes they built to act as a symbol that Christ is the foundation of their lives and property.

Step 9: Fill Your Home with Glory

You are to fill your home with objects and activities that bring glory to God. Jack Hayford offers this list of six practices that promote healthy, happy, holy homes:

1. Take Communion with your family at home. Be sure to include the children.
2. Sing at home, both alone and together. Let your home be filled with the song of the Lord.

3. Pray at home. Pray as a family. Make table prayer meaningful, even though it is brief. Scheduled times of prayer are great, but so is prayer that rises naturally, and it helps the kids enter in as genuine participants instead of being forced.

4. Testify about the good things God has done for you at home. Dinnertime is a great time to talk about what Jesus did to help you today.

5. Speak the Word in your house. Besides your own devotional Bible reading, how about standing in the center of your living room periodically and reading a psalm aloud?

6. Keep your house bright. Cultivate a genuine mood of hope in your home. Refuse whatever influences (moodiness, sharp speech, unworthy music, activities or videos) would extinguish the brightness of God's glory light in your home.[4]

Step 10: Maintain Spiritual Victory

Keep on your toes! The enemy loves to find new and creative ways of infiltrating your home with spiritual darkness. It is a good idea to go through your home periodically and check for any new objects that should not be in your home, or pray through any new sin issues that have come up. In addition, plan on consecrating the rooms of your house and walking the perimeters of your property at least once a year. You might want to pick a day (such as Good Friday) that will remind you each year that the time has come to do a spiritual checkup and to rededicate your house to the Lord.

May the Lord richly bless you as you seek to protect your home from spiritual darkness and to live the glory of His presence!

Notes

1. Pat Robertson, "Spiritual Answers to Hard Questions," *The Spirit-Filled Life Bible* (Nashville, TN: Thomas Nelson, 1991), p. 1997.

2. Charles H. Kraft, *Defeating Dark Angels* (Ann Arbor, MI: Servant Publications, 1992), p. 43.

3. Bob Beckett has written about staking a whole community in his book *Commitment to Conquer* (Chosen Books, 1997), which is an excellent resource for further study.

4. Jack Hayford, *Glory on Your House* (Grand Rapids, MI: Chosen Books, 1991), pp. 94-104.

PRAYER OF RELEASE FOR FREEMASONS AND THEIR DESCENDANTS

If you were once a member of a Masonic organization or are a descendant of someone who was, we recommend that you pray through this prayer from your heart. Don't be like the Masons who are given their obligations and oaths one line at a time and without prior knowledge of the requirements. Please read it through first so that you know what is involved. It is best to pray this aloud with a Christian witness or counselor present. We suggest a brief pause following each paragraph to allow the Holy Spirit to show any related issues, which may require attention.

Father God, creator of heaven and earth, I come to you in the name of Jesus Christ your Son. I come as a sinner seeking forgiveness and cleansing from all sins committed against you and others made in your image. I honor my earthly father and mother and all of my ancestors of flesh and blood, and of the spirit by adoption and godparents, but I utterly turn away from and renounce all their sins. I forgive all my ancestors for the effects of their sins on me and my children. I confess and renounce all of my own sins. I renounce and rebuke Satan and every spiritual power of his affecting me and my family.

In the name of the Lord Jesus Christ, I renounce and forsake all involvement in Freemasonry or any other lodge, craft or occultism by my ancestors and myself. I also renounce and break the code of silence enforced by Freemasonry and the occult on my family and myself. I renounce and repent of all pride and arrogance, which opened the door for the slavery and bondage of Freemasonry to afflict my family and me. I now shut every door of witchcraft and deception operating in my life and seal it closed with the blood of the Lord Jesus Christ. I renounce every covenant, every blood covenant and every alliance with Freemasonry or the spiritual powers behind it made by my family or me.

In the name of Jesus Christ, I renounce and cut off witchcraft, the principal spirit behind Freemasonry, and I renounce and cut off Baphomet, the Spirit of Antichrist and the spirits of Death and Deception. I renounce the insecurity, the love of position and power, the love of money, avarice or greed, and the pride, which would have led my ancestors into Masonry. I renounce all the fears that held them in Masonry, especially the fears of death, fears of men and fears of trusting, in the name of Jesus Christ.

I renounce every position held in the lodge by any of my ancestors or myself, including "Master," "Worshipful Master," or any other. I renounce the calling of any man "Master," for Jesus Christ is my only master and Lord, and He forbids anyone else having that title. I renounce the entrapping of others into Masonry, and observing the helplessness of others during the rituals. I renounce the effects of Masonry passed on to me through any female ancestor who felt distrusted and rejected by her husband as he entered and attended any lodge and refused to tell her of his secret activities.

First Degree

I renounce the oaths taken and the curses and iniquities involved in the First or Entered Apprentice Degree, especially their effects on the throat and tongue. I renounce the Hoodwink blindfold and its effects on spirit, emotions and eyes, including all confusion, fear of the dark, fear of the light and fear of sudden noises. . . . I renounce the secret word, BOAZ, *and its Masonic meaning. . . . I renounce the mixing and mingling of truth and error . . . and the blasphemy of this degree of Masonry. . . . I renounce the cable tow noose around the neck, the fear of choking and also every spirit causing asthma, hay fever, emphysema or any other breathing difficulty. I renounce the ritual dagger, or the compass point, sword or spear held against the breast, the fear of death by stabbing pain and the fear of heart attack from this degree. . . . I now pray for healing of . . .* [throat, vocal cords, nasal passages, sinus, bronchial tubes etc.] *and for healing of the speech area, and the release of the Word of God to me and through me and my family.*

Second Degree

I renounce the oaths taken and the curses and iniquities involved in the Second or Fellow Craft Degree of Masonry, especially the curses on the heart and chest. I renounce the secret words SHIBBOLETH *and* JACHIN *and all their Masonic meaning. . . . I cut off emotional hardness, apathy, indifference, unbelief and deep anger from me and my family. In the name of Jesus Christ, I pray for the healing of . . .* [the chest/lung/heart area] *and also for the healing of my emotions, and I ask to be made sensitive to the Holy Spirit of God.*

Third Degree

I renounce the oaths taken and the curses and iniquities involved in the Third or Master Mason Degree, especially the curses on the stomach and womb area. I renounce the secret words TUBAL CAIN *and* MAHA BONE *and all their Masonic meaning. . . . I renounce the Spirit of Death from the blows to the head enacted as ritual murder, the fear of death, false martyrdom, fear of violent gang attack, assault, or rape, and the helplessness of this degree. I renounce the falling into the coffin or stretcher involved in the ritual of murder. . . . I renounce the false resurrection of this degree, because only Jesus Christ is the Resurrection and the Life! (I also renounce the blasphemous kissing of the Bible on a witchcraft oath. I cut off all spirits of death, witchcraft and deception.) In the name of Jesus Christ, I pray for the healing of . . .* [the stomach, gallbladder, womb, liver and any other organ of my body affected by Masonry], *and I ask for a release of compassion and understanding for me and my family.*

Holy Royal Arch Degree

I renounce and forsake the oaths taken and the curses and iniquities involved in the Holy Royal Arch Degree, especially the oath regarding the removal of the head from the body and the exposing of the brains to the hot sun. (I renounce the Mark Lodge, and the mark in the form of squares and angles, which marks the person for life. I also reject the jewel or talisman, which may have been made from this mark sign and worn at lodge meetings.) I renounce the false secret name of God, JAHBULON, and declare total rejection of all worship of the false pagan gods, Bul or Baal, and On or Osiris. I also renounce the password AMMI RUHAMAH and all its Masonic meaning. I renounce the false communion taken in this degree, and all the mockery, skepticism and unbelief about the redemptive work of Jesus Christ on the cross of Calvary. I cut off all these curses and their effects on me and my family in the name of Jesus Christ, and I pray for healing of . . . [the brain, the mind, etc.].

Eighteenth Degree

I renounce the oaths taken and the curses, iniquities and penalties involved in the Eighteenth Degree of Masonry, the Most Wise Sovereign Knight of the Pelican and the Eagle and Sovereign Prince Rose Croix of Heredom. I renounce and reject the Pelican witchcraft spirit, as well as the occultic influence of the Rosicrucians and the Cabbala in this degree.

I renounce the claim that the death of Jesus Christ was a "dire calamity," and also the deliberate mockery and twisting of the Christian doctrine of the Atonement. I renounce the blasphemy and rejection of the deity of Jesus Christ, and the secret words IGNE NATURA RENOVATUR INTEGRA and its burning. I renounce the mockery of the Communion taken in this degree, including a biscuit, salt and white wine.

Thirtieth Degree

I renounce the oaths taken and the curses and iniquities involved in the Thirtieth Degree of Masonry, the Grand Knight Kadosh and Knight of the Black and White Eagle. I renounce the secret passwords STIBIUM ALKABAR, PHARASH-KOH and all they mean.

Thirty-First Degree

I renounce the oaths taken and the curses and iniquities involved in the Thirty-First Degree of Masonry, the Grand Inspector Inquisitor Commander. I renounce all the gods and goddesses of Egypt, which are honored in this degree, including Anubis with the jackal's head, Osiris the sun god, Isis, the sister and wife of Osiris, and also the moon goddess. I renounce the Soul of Cheres, the false symbol of immortality, the chamber of the dead and the false teaching of reincarnation.

Thirty-Second Degree

I renounce the oaths taken and the curses and iniquities involved in the Thirty-Second Degree of Masonry, the Sublime Prince of the Royal Secret. . . . I renounce Masonry's false trinitarian deity AUM, and its parts: Brahma the creator, Vishnu the preserver and Shiva the destroyer. I renounce the deity of AHURA-MAZDA, the claimed spirit or source of all light, and the worship with fire, which is an abomination to God, and also the drinking from a human skull in many rites.

York Rite

I renounce and forsake the oaths taken and the curses and iniquities involved in the York Rite Degrees of Masonry. (These include Mark Master, Past Master, Most Excellent Master, Royal Master, Select Master, Super Excellent Master, the Orders of the Red Cross, the Knights of Malta and the Knights Templar degrees. I renounce the secret words JOPPA, KEB RAIOTH *and* MAHER-SHALAL-HASH-BAZ. *I renounce the vows taken on a human skull, the crossed swords, and the curse and death wish of Judas—having the head cut off and placed on top of a church spire. I renounce the unholy communion and especially drinking from a human skull in many rites.)*

Shriners (Applies Only in North America)

I renounce the oaths taken and the curses, iniquities and penalties involved in the Ancient Arabic Order of the Nobles of the Mystic Shrine. I renounce the piercing of the eyeballs with a three-edged blade, the flaying of the feet, the madness and the worship of the false god Allah as the god of our fathers. I renounce the hoodwink, the mock hanging, the mock beheading, the mock drinking of the blood of the victim, the mock dog urinating on the initiate, and the offering of urine as a commemoration.

Thirty-Third and Supreme Degree

I renounce the oaths taken and the curses and iniquities involved in the supreme Thirty-Third Degree of Freemasonry, the Grand Sovereign Inspector General. . . . I renounce and utterly forsake The Great Architect of the Universe, who is revealed in this degree as Lucifer, and his false claim to be the universal fatherhood of God. I renounce the cable tow around the neck. I renounce the death wish that the wine drunk from a human skull should turn to poison and the skeleton whose cold arms are invited if the oath of this degree is violated. I renounce the three infamous assassins of their grand master, law, property and religion, and the greed and witchcraft involved in the attempt to manipulate and control the rest of mankind.

All Other Degrees

I renounce all the other oaths taken, the rituals of every other degree and the curses and iniquities involved. These include the Allied Degrees, The Red Cross of Constantine, the order of the Secret Monitor, and the Masonic Royal Order of Scotland. I renounce all other lodges and secret societies including Prince Hall Freemasonry, Grand Orient Lodges, Mormonism, the Order of Amaranth, the Royal Order of Jesters, the Manchester Unity Order of Odd Fellows, Buffalos, Druids, Foresters, the Loyal Orange, Black and Purple Lodges, Elks, Moose and Eagles Lodges, the Ku Klux Klan, the Grange, the Woodmen of the World, Riders of the Red Robe, the Knights of Pythias, the Mystic Order of the Veiled Prophets of the Enchanted Realm; the women's Orders of the Eastern Star, Ladies Oriental Shrine, and White Shrine of Jerusalem; the girls' Orders of the Daughters of the Eastern Star, Job's Daughters, and Rainbow; and the boys' Order of DeMolay, and their effects on me and all my family.

(I renounce the ancient pagan teaching and symbolism of the First Tracing Board, the Second Tracing Board and the Third Tracing Board used in the ritual of the Blue Lodge. I renounce the pagan ritual of the "Point within a Circle" with all its bondages and phallus worship. I renounce the occultic mysticism of the black and white mosaic checkered floor with the tessellated border and five-pointed blazing star. I renounce the symbol "G" and its veiled pagan symbolism and bondages. I also renounce the false claim that Lucifer is the Morning Star and Shining One, and I declare that Jesus Christ is the Bright and Morning Star of Revelation 22:16.)

I renounce the All-Seeing Third Eye of Freemasonry or Horus in the forehead and its pagan and occult symbolism. . . . I renounce all false communions taken, all mockery of the redemptive work of Jesus Christ on the cross of Calvary, all unbelief, confusion and depression (and all worship of Lucifer as God). I renounce and forsake the lie of Freemasonry that man is not sinful, but merely imperfect, and so he can redeem himself through good works. I rejoice that the Bible states that I cannot do a single thing to earn my salvation, but that I can only be saved by grace through faith in Jesus Christ and what He accomplished on the cross of Calvary.

I renounce all fear of insanity, anguish, death wishes, suicide and death in the name of Jesus Christ. Jesus Christ conquered death, and He alone holds the keys of death and hell, and I rejoice that He holds my life in His hands now. He came to give me life abundantly and eternally, and I believe His promises.

I renounce all anger, hatred, murderous thoughts, revenge, retaliation, spiritual apathy, false religion, all unbelief, especially unbelief in the Holy Bible as God's Word, and all compromise of God's Word. I renounce all spiritual searching into false religions and all striving to please God. I rest in the knowledge that I have found my Lord and Savior Jesus Christ and that He has found me.

I will burn or destroy all objects in my possession that connect me with all lodges and occultic organizations, including Masonry, witchcraft and Mormonism, and all regalia, aprons, books of rituals, rings and other jewelry. I renounce the effects these or other objects of Masonry, including the compass and the square, (the noose or the blindfold) have had on me or my family, in the name of Jesus Christ.

All participants should now be invited to sincerely carry out in faith the following 10 actions:

1. symbolically remove the blindfold (hoodwink) and give it to the Lord for disposal;
2. in the same way, symbolically remove the veil of mourning, to make way to receive the joy of the Lord;
3. symbolically cut and remove the noose from around the neck, gather it up with the cable tow running down the body and give it all to the Lord for His disposal;
4. renounce the false Freemasonry marriage covenant, removing from the fourth finger of the right hand the ring of this false marriage covenant, giving it to the Lord to dispose of it;
5. symbolically remove the chains and bondages of Freemasonry from your body.
6. symbolically remove all Freemasonry regalia, including collars, gauntlets and armor, especially the Apron with its snake clasp, to make way for the Belt of Truth;
7. remove the slipshod slippers to make way for the shoes of the Gospel of Peace;
8. invite participants to repent of and seek forgiveness having walked on all unholy ground, including Freemasonry lodges and temples, and any Mormon or other occultic/Masonic organizations;
9. symbolically remove the ball and chain from the ankles;
10. proclaim that Satan and his demons no longer have any legal rights to mislead and manipulate the person seeking help.

Holy Spirit, I ask that You show me anything else, which I need to do or to pray so that I and my family may be totally free from the consequences of the sins of Masonry, witchcraft, Mormonism and all related paganism and occultism.

Pause, while listening to God, and pray as the Holy Spirit leads you:

Now, dear Father God, I ask humbly for the blood of Jesus Christ, Your Son and my Savior, to cleanse me from all these sins I have confessed and renounced: to cleanse my spirit, my soul, my mind, my emotions and every part of my body which has been affected by these sins, in the name of Jesus Christ.

(I renounce every evil spirit associated with Masonry and witchcraft, and all other sins, and I command in the name of Jesus Christ for Satan and every evil spirit to be bound and to leave me now, touching or harming no one, and to go to the place appointed for you by the Lord Jesus, never to return to my family or me. I call on the name of the Lord Jesus to be delivered of these spirits, in accordance with the many promises of the Bible. I ask to be delivered of every spirit of sickness, infirmity, curse, affliction, addiction, disease or allergy associated with these sins I have confessed and renounced. I surrender to God's Holy Spirit and to no other spirit all the places in my life where these sins have been.) I ask you, Lord, to baptize me, fill me anew with Your Holy Spirit now according to the promises in Your Word. I take to myself the whole armor of God in accordance with Ephesians 6 and rejoice in its protection as Jesus surrounds me and fills me with His Holy Spirit. I enthrone You, Lord Jesus, in my heart, for You are my Lord and my Savior, the source of eternal life. Thank You, Father God, for Your mercy, Your forgiveness and Your love, in the name of Jesus Christ, amen.

Source

This prayer is taken from Dr. Selwyn Stevens, *Unmasking Freemasonry—Removing the Hoodwink* (Wellington, New Zealand: Jubilee Publishers, n.d.).

Copying of this prayer is both permitted and encouraged provided reference is made to where it comes from: Jubilee Resources, PO Box 36-044, Wellington 6330, New Zealand (ISBN 1877203-48-3). Copies of *Unmasking Freemasonry* as well as this prayer can be found at http://www.jubileeresourcesusa.org.

Written testimonies of changed lives and healings are welcome. If additional prayer and ministry are required, or information is required about other spiritual deceptions, please contact Jubilee Resources. For reasons of distance, Jubilee Resources may refer you to someone based closer to you.

RECOMMENDED READING

Beckett, Bob, with Rebecca Wagner Sytsema. *Commitment to Conquer*. Grand Rapids, MI: Chosen Books, 1997.
Discusses strategic level spiritual warfare from the perspective of a local church pastor. Offers excellent understanding of issues regarding land and property.

Gibson, Noel and Phyl. *Deliver Our Children from the Evil One*. Ventura, CA: Renew Books, 1992.
Offers both preventative and therapeutic solutions to defend children against satanic attacks.

————. *Evicting Demonic Intruders*. West Sussex, England: New Wine Press, 1993.
Used by Doris M. Wagner, deliverance concentration coordinator for Wagner Leadership Institute, as her main text for deliverance seminars. Offers some of the best insight and advice for ministering freedom from demonic forces.

Hammond, Frank D. and Ida Mae. *Pigs in the Parlor*. Kirkwood, MO: Impact Christian Books, 1973.
One of the standard books on deliverance, which has been in print for over 25 years and has been helpful to many as an introduction to and handbook for casting out demons.

————. *A Manual for Children's Deliverance*. Kirkwood, MO: Impact Christian Books, 1996.
A sequel to *Pigs in the Parlor*, this book is designed to deal specifically with evil influences and deliverance methods for children.

Horrobin, Peter. *Healing Through Deliverance I: The Biblical Basis*. Ventura, CA: Renew Books, 1991.
Offers a comprehensive assessment of the place of deliverance ministry in the life of the church.

————. *Healing Through Deliverance II: The Practical Ministry*. Ventura, CA: Renew Books, 1995.
This companion volume to the above book provides important foundational material for ministering healing and deliverance.

Jacobs, Cindy. *Possessing the Gates of the Enemy*. Grand Rapids, MI: Baker Books, 1994.
Lives up to its subtitle: "A Training Manual for Militant Intercession." It has a wealth of information on prayer found in no other source.

Kraft, Charles H. *I Give You Authority*. Grand Rapids, MI: Chosen Books, 1997.
This shows how to properly exercise the authority we have been given through the Holy Spirit in order to transform our lives and be free from satanic oppression.

———. *Defeating Dark Angels*. Ventura, CA: Regal Books, 2004.
This book is a thorough and practical manual on personal deliverance from demons by a Fuller Theological Seminary professor who draws from a wide experience.

MacNutt, Francis. *Deliverance from Evil Spirits*. Grand Rapids, MI: Chosen Books, 1995.
This book is a highly recommended, practical manual on casting out demons.

Murphy, Ed. *The Handbook for Spiritual Warfare*. Nashville, TN: Thomas Nelson, 1996.
This is the most exhaustive textbook on spiritual warfare available. It is very strong on biblical material.

Pierce, Chuck D., and Rebecca Wagner Sytsema. *Possessing Your Inheritance*. Ventura, CA: Regal Books, 1999.
Offers clear principles for Christian living, which help the reader understand and possess their inheritance in the Lord. Includes an extensive chapter on generational sin and iniquity.

———. *The Best Is Yet Ahead*. Colorado Springs, CO: Wagner Publications, 2001.

———. *Restoring Your Shield of Faith*. Ventura, CA: Regal Books, 2003.

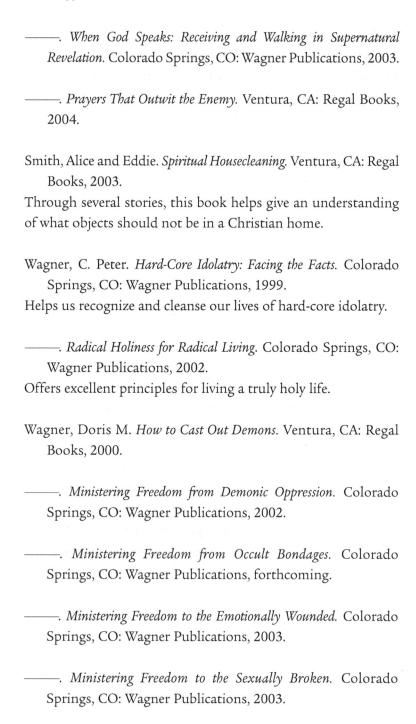

————. *When God Speaks: Receiving and Walking in Supernatural Revelation.* Colorado Springs, CO: Wagner Publications, 2003.

————. *Prayers That Outwit the Enemy.* Ventura, CA: Regal Books, 2004.

Smith, Alice and Eddie. *Spiritual Housecleaning.* Ventura, CA: Regal Books, 2003.
Through several stories, this book helps give an understanding of what objects should not be in a Christian home.

Wagner, C. Peter. *Hard-Core Idolatry: Facing the Facts.* Colorado Springs, CO: Wagner Publications, 1999.
Helps us recognize and cleanse our lives of hard-core idolatry.

————. *Radical Holiness for Radical Living.* Colorado Springs, CO: Wagner Publications, 2002.
Offers excellent principles for living a truly holy life.

Wagner, Doris M. *How to Cast Out Demons.* Ventura, CA: Regal Books, 2000.

————. *Ministering Freedom from Demonic Oppression.* Colorado Springs, CO: Wagner Publications, 2002.

————. *Ministering Freedom from Occult Bondages.* Colorado Springs, CO: Wagner Publications, forthcoming.

————. *Ministering Freedom to the Emotionally Wounded.* Colorado Springs, CO: Wagner Publications, 2003.

————. *Ministering Freedom to the Sexually Broken.* Colorado Springs, CO: Wagner Publications, 2003.

White, Thomas B. *The Believer's Guide to Spiritual Warfare*. Ventura, CA: Regal Books, 2004.
Offers excellent material on our personal preparation for spiritual warfare.

CPSIA information can be obtained
at www.ICGtesting.com
Printed in the USA
LVHW081316121122
732996LV00015B/1093